The Cake the Buddha Ate

More QUIET FOOD

Chrisi van Loon   Louis van Loon
Daniel Jardim   Angela Shaw
Dorian Haarhoff   Stephen Coan
Claire Clark

JACANA

First published by Jacana Media (Pty) Ltd in 2011
10 Orange Street
Sunnyside
Auckland Park 2092
South Africa
+2711 628 3200
www.jacana.co.za

ISBN 978-1-77009-772-8

Edited by: Chrisi van Loon
Photographs by: Angela Shaw; Tomas Campher, front cover,
    pp ii, 4, 36, 98, 116, 122, 146, 150; Rodney Kidd, p 92.
Set in Sabon 10.5/16pt
Printed and bound by Craft Print International Ltd
Job No. 001404

See a complete list of Jacana titles at www.jacana.co.za

Contents

The cake the Buddha ate

Daniel Jardim, our chef at the Buddhist Retreat Centre, had had a difficult day. So had Anthony Shapiro, the master potter who worked and lived there for about two years. It had been "one of those days", so to console themselves Daniel whipped up their favourite dessert, carrot cake, only to be faced with a power outage! When your kiln or oven goes dead in the middle of firing your bowls or baking your favourite cake, you too would get a little grumpy. Even at a meditation centre.

The cake took two hours to bake slowly in the remaining heat of the oven, but came out perfectly. It was iced in torch light. They took it to their kutis on the edge of the forest where they had a slice each. Carrot cake had never tasted better. In the failing light the remainder was cut into further wedges, to be offered to the rest of the staff in the morning. The cake was covered. They went to bed.

Upon waking, Daniel noticed that a slice of cake had gone missing during the night. The cake's gauze cover had not been disturbed. Puzzled, he looked around his room. His gaze came to rest on the little shrine he had created which had a small bronze Buddha statue at its centre. The Buddha's beautiful smile seemed a little coy in the early morning light. Looking closer, he noticed a smudge on the side of the Buddha's mouth.

It was icing sugar.

This is not just another recipe book

Let's face it, there are enough recipe books weighing down the shelves of book shops. Why publish yet another one?

It is true that this book is different in that it features exclusively vegetarian dishes. Still, you will find other vegetarian cook books on those shelves. So, what makes this recipe book so special that it deserves a place amongst dozens of other titles?

Well, for a start, these recipes are particularly inventive, tasty and nutritious, honed to perfection by a very talented cook, who happens to have been a vegetarian from an early age. Also, they were created at a meditation centre, the Buddhist Retreat Centre (BRC) in Ixopo, KwaZulu-Natal, South Africa, where we eat our food in "Noble Silence" – to better savour and appreciate the finer points of this type of cooking. You are the beneficiary of this additional contemplative dimension given to these dishes. If you close your eyes, you can taste it.

You cannot separate the food from the place. We have therefore given you an additional flavour in this recipe book: the feel of the BRC. The photographs of its beautiful environs and the intriguing activities taking place there are evidence that we do more than eat great food at the BRC.

5

To be or not to be a vegetarian LOUIS VAN LOON

It was March 1956, barely ten years after the end of the Second World War. I had emigrated to South Africa only a few months earlier from Holland. I had just turned twenty-one.

Shortly after arriving in Durban, I ordered lunch at the IXL tearoom on the beach front. The dish looked innocent enough. I ordered it principally because it included mashed potatoes. I loved mashed potatoes. Still do. When it arrived at my table, it had something alongside the mash that intrigued me. I called the waiter and asked him what it was. "Cutlet," he said. "Cutlet," and walked off. Waiters weren't very forthcoming at the IXL.

I looked at the bone sticking out of the meat and felt queasy. That must have once belonged to an animal, I thought. It was a piece from a corpse. I was expected to eat that. I paid and left my dish untouched. Even the mashed potatoes.

As I walked back to my flat on the Marine Parade, I pondered my experience. I had occasionally eaten meat in Holland, of course. But not like that. Meat had been very scarce, and costly, during and after the war. When it was available, it was mostly dressed up as sausages or slices of bacon wrapped in a packet with a smiling pig's face on it. Or tinned corned beef. The content tasted nice. That was all there was to it. It was a nice taste.

In South Africa I had continued with the diet I had got used to in Holland. Mostly bread and cheese, vegetables and fruit. And mashed potatoes. But that bone confronted me with the stark reality of meat-eating. I remembered great historical figures I admired who had chosen to be vegetarian: Tolstoy, Plotinus, Leonardo da Vinci, Gandhi, Bernard Shaw. I decided to join their ranks.

But it was not easy to be a vegetarian in South Africa in those days. The Sunday braai was – still is – a sacrosanct national institution. But I decided to take that bull by the horns, so to speak, and started a campaign to promote the advantages, and ethics, of being vegetarian in a series of deliberately confrontational articles in newspapers and magazines. People started to take notice. Vegetarian societies sprung up. Health food stores opened. Rather than looking at you as if you were a visitor from another galaxy, restaurants began to feature vegetarian dishes.

At about the same time I travelled widely to study Buddhist philosophy and visit monasteries and meditation centres in the east and west. My one overwhelming experience was the unpalatable, unhealthy food they offered – particularly those claiming to adhere to a vegetarian diet. Rice gruel cooked in coconut milk; nut roasts that could sink a battleship – that sort of thing. So when it came to opening the Buddhist Retreat Centre in Ixopo, in 1980, one of my main concerns was to make its kitchen a showpiece of excellent vegetarian cooking.

I think we have succeeded in doing this. For many of our visitors it comes as a revelation that vegetarian dishes can be that tasty, varied and nutritious.

Almost from the beginning we were asked for recipes of our dishes. These were first written out on paper serviettes. They were then photocopied and stapled together into our first recipe book. This morphed into some home-spun publications with cute names like *Just Cook It* and *Essie in the Kitchen*. Then came our big moment: *Quiet Food: A Recipe for Sanity* was published in 2005 and became a surprising success. It is now in its fifth reprint and still in demand.

This collection of recipes, *The Cake the Buddha Ate: More Quiet Food*, aims to take this vegetarian journey yet further. The dishes in this book were honed to perfection by Daniel Jardim, who was our chef at the Buddhist Retreat Centre for two years and still teaches cookery workshops there. Daniel clearly has cooking talent embedded in his genes. His grandparents were cooks. His parents run a cookery school in Johannesburg.

Daniel studied Holistic Nutrition in London, worked in restaurants there and researched the interface between our health and the environment and the season we happen to be living in.

It became obvious that we should immortalise his culinary creations in another collection of recipes.

This book is the result.

Of recipes and retreats DANIEL JARDIM

It's Friday evening at the Buddhist Retreat Centre; the beginning of a weekend retreat. Guests are arriving. Some are here for the first time, a little apprehensive perhaps, not quite knowing what to expect, even though their friends have raved about the place. Others show that easy confidence that comes from knowing the Centre well, having visited it so many times. They greet each other like long-lost friends. But soon the newcomers, too, relax into the friendly, serene feel of the Centre.

I have cooked mixed vegetable and barley soup for them tonight. It is going to be served with freshly-baked farm bread. As the guests help themselves to bowls of steaming soup, it strikes me that the story of the soup is just like the stories our visitors are exchanging.

Some of the ingredients are as familiar as the friends we see every day. We start with such basics as an onion, a carrot, a handful of chopped parsley – those wonderful, dependable staples of cooking. Next, we add the barley and some seasonable vegetables, some of which we have not been able to get for a while and only arrived with the afternoon delivery. Then there may be those ingredients that we are using for the first time: fresh leeks that have been growing quietly in the garden; a new kind of squash as their companion; a daring pinch of spice which we would not normally add, but which seemed like a good idea at the time.

As the guests settle down to their meal, there is a palpable sense of communion that mealtimes bring. People meeting at retreats are like ingredients blending. Personalities are like flavours, each one enriching the other in mysterious, often unpredictable ways. Retreats are like recipes – a medium that enables stimulating interactions to happen.

When we eat a meal together with others, we share a deeply embedded human need. This must be because food is so basic to our physical survival. When we eat with others, we instinctively bond to them in our quintessential humanness.

We can, of course, feel this bond with all creatures. Maybe this is what inclines some of us to be vegetarian. Because, as vegetarians, we step away from eating our fellow creatures. We leave them alone to find their own way in life. That feels good.

I hope that this book will inspire you towards that same sentiment and that you will find as much fulfillment in cooking these recipes as I had creating them.

soups

a warm welcome

mixed vegetable and barley soup

(serves 4)

A perennial favourite at the Centre. Warmth, comfort and nourishment mingle together in one pot. The combination of onion, leeks, carrots and celery, together with a hint of fresh herbs, makes the perfect base for any vegetable soup and eliminates the need to use commercial stocks, which are often laden with synthetic ingredients. Soaking the barley beforehand reduces the cooking time and produces a thick and velvety soup. To make a clearer soup, cook the barley separately and add before serving.

olive oil
1 onion, chopped
2 garlic cloves, chopped
2 leeks, finely sliced
2 celery stalks, finely chopped
1 tbsp fresh rosemary, finely chopped
½ cup fresh parsley, chopped
2 carrots, chopped
2 baby marrows, chopped
1 turnip, peeled and chopped
1 potato, peeled and cubed
1 cup green beans, chopped
½ cup barley, rinsed and soaked in
    cold water (1 hour at least)
salt and pepper to taste

Sauté the onion in a small amount of oil. Add the garlic, leeks, celery and herbs and stir for a further 2 minutes.

Add the carrots and continue to stir until the onion is translucent.

Mix in the remaining ingredients and cover with water.

Simmer gently until the barley is tender.

Adjust the seasoning and serve.

Tip

When making the soup, it is often difficult to gauge how much water to add. Often recipes include a set amount of water which sometimes results in a soup that is far too watery and bland. To achieve the best consistency, always add enough water to just cover the vegetables. This ensures the best results; you can always add a splash of water if you feel the soup is too thick.

Never boil soup. It destroys the delicate flavours and makes burning more likely. Always add cold water to soups – bring the pot to the boil and then reduce to simmer gently until cooked.

smooth summer silk

carrot, apple and celery soup

A light and delicate soup that can be served hot or cold. Any type of apple can be used; choose red for a sweeter soup or green for a slightly sharper flavour.

Sauté the onion in the oil. Add the leeks, carrots, celery, ginger and half of the parsley, and stir over a low heat for 2 to 3 minutes, adding a little extra water if necessary.

Add the apples and potatoes. Cover with water and simmer until the vegetables are tender.

Blend until smooth and silky.

Adjust the seasoning.

Add the remaining parsley before serving.

10 ml vegetable oil

1 onion, chopped

2 leeks, chopped

6 carrots, scrubbed and chopped

1 bunch celery, chopped

2 tbsp ginger, grated

½ cup chopped parsley

2 apples, peeled, cored and sliced

2 potatoes, peeled and chopped

salt and pepper to taste

17

broccoli bisque

cream of broccoli soup

(serves 4)

The combination of yoghurt and milk in this recipe produces a thick and creamy soup without the heavy richness of cream. Simmer the broccoli until just tender for the best flavour.

Sauté the onion in butter on a low heat until soft and transparent.

Remove from the heat and add just enough flour to form a thick paste.

Return to the heat and slowly add water to form a thick liquid.

Add the broccoli and tomato; season with salt and pepper, and add just enough water to cover.

Simmer gently for 20 to 30 minutes. Blend until smooth.

Add the milk, yoghurt and dill just before serving.

1 onion, chopped
50 g butter
50 ml nutty wheat (or wholemeal flour)
1 head broccoli, chopped
1 small tomato, chopped
salt and pepper to taste
water (approx. 2 cups)
125 ml milk
125 ml yoghurt
1 tsp dried dill

19

junaq's gem

gem squash and sweet potato soup

(serves 4)

Gem squashes are in such plentiful supply in this country and yet they are generally, unimaginatively, served steamed with the most meager of seasonings. This simple soup was inspired by Junaq who has lived and worked at the Centre for almost thirty years. She encouraged us to create something a little different with the bounty of gem squashes that we always had available. Its light texture and delicate flavour make it an excellent soup for warm summery days.

Sauté the onion with cumin and cinnamon in the oil until tender. Add the ginger and celery, and fry for a further 3 minutes.

Add the gem squash and sweet potato and cover with water. Simmer gently until the sweet potato is cooked.

Blend until smooth.

Adjust seasoning and add chopped coriander before serving.

10 ml vegetable oil
1 onion, chopped
1 tsp cumin seeds
1 cinnamon stick
15 ml ginger, grated
1 celery stalk, chopped
2 cups gem squash pulp
2 large sweet potatoes, chopped
salt and pepper to taste
15 ml fresh coriander, chopped

golden lights

cauliflower and butternut soup with za'atar dressing

It is unusual to make a dressing for a soup, but in this case, it really helps to lift all the delicate flavours of this autumn soup. Za'atar is a Middle-Eastern seasoning made with thyme and sesame seeds. We have added a little lemon to ours for extra zing.

Sauté the onion with the spices in a little oil or water. Add the leeks, celery and garlic and sauté for 3 to 4 minutes until the onion is translucent.

Add the remaining ingredients and enough water to cover the ingredients.

Simmer for 15 to 20 minutes until all the vegetables are tender.

Remove from the heat.

Remove the cinnamon and blend until smooth.

For the dressing, combine all the ingredients, and stir into the soup just before serving.

Adjust the seasoning.

15 ml vegetable oil
1 onion, chopped
1 stick cinnamon
1 tsp cumin seeds
1 tsp coriander seeds
½ tsp coriander, ground
2 cloves
2 leeks, sliced
1 celery stalk, chopped
2 garlic cloves
1 cauliflower, (about 600 g) chopped
1 potato, peeled and chopped
2 cups butternut, (about 400 g) chopped
salt and pepper to taste

za'atar dressing
½ cup parsley, finely chopped
1 tbsp fresh thyme
1 garlic clove, finely chopped
1 tbsp olive oil
1 tbsp lemon juice
60 ml sesame seeds, toasted
salt and pepper to taste

21

mantet mellit

sweet potato and cumin soup

(serves 4)

The name of this Thai-influenced soup is a rough translation of its two key ingredients, namely sweet potato and cumin. Potatoes come in all shapes and sizes, so measurements for this soup do not need to be exact. As a general rule, remember to use approximately equal amounts of potato as sweet potato. If you are using coconut cream from a tin, add approximately half a tin as part of the cooking liquid.

Heat the oil and sauté the cumin seeds. Add the onion and cook until it is soft and translucent.

Mix in the ginger, garlic and cumin powder and fry for a further minute.

Add the diced potato, sweet potato, seasoning and stock cube, and enough water to cover.

Simmer gently for 30 minutes until the potato is tender.

Blend very well until the soup is thick and velvety.

Return to the heat. Add more water, if needed.

Once the soup has warmed through, stir in the coconut cream and coriander.

Add the garam masala just before serving.

15 ml olive oil
1 tsp cumin seeds
1 onion, chopped
2 tsp grated ginger
2 garlic cloves, crushed
1 tsp ground cumin
3 potatoes, peeled and cubed
1 large sweet potato, peeled and cubed
1 vegetable stock cube
salt and pepper to taste
2-3 tbsp coconut cream powder
½ cup fresh coriander, roughly chopped
pinch of garam masala

Tip
Coconut cream powder is available at most Asian supermarkets. It is convenient to use for recipes that require a smaller amount of coconut without having to open a large tin.

23

andalucian antics

red pepper and tomato soup

A feast of fiery Mediterranean flavours. As a variation, replace the parsley with basil or coriander. If you are wary of the soup being too hot, add the chillies whole and then remove them from the soup when the spicy taste is to your liking.

Sauté the onion in oil and butter until translucent.

Add the tinned tomatoes, carrots, celery, chillies and peppers, and stir for a few minutes.

Add the potatoes, peppercorns and "normal" paprika, and cover with water. Simmer gently for 30 minutes until all the vegetables are tender.

Blend well until smooth and silky. (For a milder soup, remove the chillies before blending.)

Season to taste.

Return to the heat until piping hot, for serving, and stir in the smoked paprika and the basil or parsley.

Serve with a drizzle of virgin olive oil.

(serves 4)

2 onions, chopped
I tbsp butter
1 tbsp olive oil
2 tins whole tomatoes
2 carrots, chopped
1 stalk celery, chopped
2 red chillies
3 red peppers, cored and
   chopped
2 medium potatoes, peeled
   and chopped
4 peppercorns
½ tsp paprika
salt and pepper to taste
pinch of smoked paprika
½ cup basil or parsley,
   chopped

mist in the wattles

spinach, potato and sweetcorn soup

A popular soup often served at the beginning of a retreat. It has a welcoming feel about it. Its earthy potato taste and just the right amount of spinach comfort and nourish our guests when they arrive – many, for the first time, having driven through the misty timber plantations that line the last stretch of road leading to the Centre. The combination of white and green pays homage to this tranquil scenery. "What about the sweetcorn?" you ask. It is a promise that the sun is sure to return.

Sauté the onion in a little olive oil until tender.

Add the garlic, ginger, rosemary and spices and stir for a further minute.

Add the potatoes, spinach and sweetcorn and cover with water.

Simmer gently until the potato is tender.

Adjust the seasoning and serve.

olive oil
1 onion, finely chopped
2 garlic cloves, minced
1 tbsp ginger, minced
1 tsp fresh rosemary, chopped
½ tsp ground coriander
½ tsp ground cumin
500 g potatoes, peeled and
  diced
½ bunch spinach, veined and
  shredded (7 to 8 large leaves)
1 cup frozen sweetcorn, rinsed
salt and pepper to taste

27

amadumbi nobontshisi

madumbi and butter bean soup

It is with delight that I see madumbis, so treasured in traditional African cooking, gaining in popularity in this country. Their flavour and texture are so unique – earthy, warming, comfortingly starchy. When they are in season we are able to order bag-fulls of them, grown by the local community, without the use of fertilisers or pesticides – straight from the earth and delivered to our kitchen door. They are so delicious and are enjoyed with nothing more than a little sea salt. This soup is a hearty and nourishing way to enjoy madumbis, together with the creamy nutty flavour of whole butter beans. Winter food at its best.

Sauté the onion in vegetable oil. Add the garlic and fry for another minute.

Add the tomatoes, celery, red pepper, paprika and peppercorns and stir until the tomato begins to soften.

Add the madumbis and cover with water. Simmer gently for 45 minutes until the madumbis are tender.

Mix in the butter beans. Heat gently until the beans are heated through. Do not boil the beans. Season to taste.

Add chopped parsley and olive oil before serving.

15 ml vegetable oil
2 onions, chopped
2 cloves garlic, crushed
1 kg red tomatoes, chopped
or 2 tins whole tomatoes
1 bunch celery, chopped
1 red pepper, cored and chopped
½ tsp paprika
4 peppercorns
1 kg madumbis, peeled and chopped
375 ml cooked butter beans (or 1 tin, drained and rinsed)
salt and pepper to taste
chopped parsley (optional)
1 tbsp olive oil

mermaid's purse soup

yellow split pea and wakame soup

With its golden split peas and seaweed, this soup is evocative of treasure found deep in the ocean. Beware of adding salt too soon because it will toughen the split peas and add another hour or so to the cooking time. Soak a little extra seaweed and cut into fine ribbons to garnish.

Sauté the onion in a little oil until translucent.

Add the garlic, celery and carrots. Cook for 2 to 3 minutes.

Add the split peas and potatoes. Cover with water. Do not add salt. Simmer for 30 minutes.

Cut the wakame into strips. Add to the soup, and simmer gently until the split peas are tender.

Season and serve.

oil for frying
2 onions, chopped
1 clove garlic, chopped
2 stalks celery, chopped
4 carrots, scrubbed and
    chopped
500 g yellow split peas,
    soaked overnight, or in hot
    water for 2 to 3 hours
2 potatoes, peeled and
    chopped
2 strips wakame seaweed,
    soaked in ice cold water for
    20 minutes
salt and pepper to taste

Tip

When cooking any pulses, it is always better to add salt towards the end of cooking so that the split peas or beans will cook faster. Adding salt in the beginning dramatically increases cooking time.

stretching up at a window
miaowing
demanding entry
someone opens the slats
   the cat squeezes through
   and finds a vacant cushion
(SC)

butter jade soup

chilled avocado and lime soup

(serves 4)

The Centre is blessed with two huge avocado trees that produce the most delicious green jewels. Every day a handful are picked and carefully wrapped, and then left to ripen in the kitchen pantry. This ensures that there are always at least a few at hand that are just ripe for eating. The thought of an avocado soup had long excited me – the problem was that even with such a bounty of fresh avocados at our disposal, they are so delicious that there were never any left when it came to making the soup. With much determination, if not a little evasion, I finally managed to make my avocado soup, and all I can say is that it was well worth the wait. The colour reminded me of the butter jade that is used in so much African sculpture and seemed the perfect moniker for this creamy, cool and velvety-smooth gem.

2 large avocados, peeled and
  mashed
1 block vegetarian soup stock,
  dissolved in 1½ cups hot water
2 tbsp lime juice
dash tabasco (optional)
½ cup liquid made up of half
  cream and half water
salt and pepper to taste
1 tbsp fresh coriander, chopped
2 tbsp sour cream
1 spring onion, finely sliced

Place the avocado, stock, lime juice and tabasco in a blender.

Gradually add the "half-and-half" cream and water, until smooth and creamy. Refrigerate.

Adjust the seasoning and add chopped coriander before serving.

Serve with a dollop of sour cream and spring onions.

31

Two-and-one-half sips of tea

During some retreats we give a demonstration of the traditional Chinese Tea Ceremony. This is more ancient and meditative than the Japanese one, which is conducted in a more ceremonial and social atmosphere. I learned the Chinese ceremony from an old Tea Master in Hong Kong in the 1960s.

The ceremony uses exquisitely shaped utensils, some of them delicately crafted out of bamboo, like the ladle, spoon and whisk. The tea bowls are raku, each uniquely marked by the haphazard way in which they survived their ordeal of fire and water.

We conduct the ceremony in our meditation hall in candlelight and burning incense, accompanied by the subdued sound of Tibetan singing bowls. The principal Tea Master performs the first round of tea-making. Four additional tea masters sit in an inner circle close to the platform where the ceremony is conducted. They take turns to perform their own version of the ceremony. Spectators watch the proceedings, sitting further back.

Everything is done slowly and in silence. The Tea Master reverently picks up each utensil and bowl and slowly turns it over to admire its craftsmanship and beauty from various angles. Everyone watches in vicarious enjoyment. He dips the bamboo ladle into a cast iron pot containing boiling water and pours some of it into the bowls. A few grains of green tea are added. The whisk is used to swirl the tea until it is dissolved. The bowls are then passed around until each member in the inner circle has one. Upon a little bow of the Master, they all drink the tea – in two-and-one-half sips.

When temple gong meets yellowwood

This ancient Chinese temple gong announces the beginning of our meditation sessions.

In April 1980, a few hours before our first visitors to the Centre were due to arrive, it struck me that we did not have a stand for it.

Then, at lunch, a friend who had helped me for a few days readying the place walked past the dining room dragging a branch from a yellowwood tree behind him. I have no idea where he had found it or why he had brought it to the Centre. But it seemed perfect to make a gong stand out of it.

I had a preconceived idea of what it should look like: cut off the straightest pieces from the branch; make these into a square frame into which the gong would hang; and mount this on some legs. This I proceeded to do. But it proved to be a time-consuming process.

As opening time approached, I looked wearily at the progress I was making and realised that it would never be finished in time. All around me lay sticks of yellowwood. The part of the tree from which these had been harvested stood there also – an oddly shaped tripod.

It was perfect to hold the gong. It needed no work whatsoever. I just hung the gong from where the branches connected. That was it. What had been rejected as useless was superior to the complicated structure I had been trying to construct. The gong stand had been there all along.

There is a lesson here somewhere.

salads

amazig-zag salad

carrot and olive platter

On one of my trips away from the Centre I managed to find a zig-zag vegetable cutter which soon became a cherished utensil amongst the kitchen staff for the unusual (and yet somehow elegant) shapes it was able to make. When we first made this Moroccan-inspired salad, it was immediately christened amazig-zag salad, after the curiously sliced carrots. I encourage you to hunt down a cutter of your own; it will guarantee endless hours of garnishing fun.

Steam the carrots until just tender and crunchy and season with olive oil, cumin, coriander, paprika, salt and pepper, toasted sesame seeds and apple cider vinegar.

Steam the green beans and season with olive oil, lemon juice and garlic just before serving.

Place the carrots on a serving dish in the centre. Arrange the green beans around the carrots, and then place olives between carrots and beans to form three layers.

Garnish with fresh herbs.

carrot layer
500 g carrots, sliced
3 tbsp olive oil
2 ml cumin, ground
2 ml coriander, ground
5 ml paprika
salt and pepper to taste
1 tbsp sesame seeds, toasted
15 ml apple cider vinegar

green bean layer
500 g green beans, sliced
15 ml olive oil
15 ml lemon juice
1 clove garlic, crushed
salt and black pepper
250 ml black olives

37

bamboo panda

broccoli and black-eyed bean salad with fennel vinaigrette

Black-eyed beans are an excellent pantry stand-by. They soak quickly and cook more rapidly than most other kinds of beans. Their decidedly "green" flavour makes them an excellent addition to salads when fresh greens are in limited supply.

Boil the beans rapidly for 10 minutes and then reduce the heat and boil until cooked. Drain.

Make the vinaigrette by combining all the ingredients. Set aside to steep.

Blanch the broccoli. Rinse in cold water and drain well.

Combine all the salad ingredients and toss well with the dressing. Adjust the seasoning and serve.

(serves 4 to 6)

39

1 cup black-eyed beans
   (soaked for at least 1 hour)
300 g broccoli florets (about
   1 head)
½ red onion, finely sliced
1 bulb fennel, sliced

fennel vinaigrette
½ cup olive oil
1-2 cloves garlic, mashed
juice of 1 lemon
2 tbsp fennel leaves, finely
   chopped
salt and pepper to taste

a mandala with jewels

beetroot, cucumber and pomegranate salad

(serves 4 to 6)

A mouth-watering and refreshing summer salad, bejewelled with ruby pomegranate seeds. Many of the salads served at the Centre are arranged, like this one, in concentric layers. The result is a dish that reminds one of a precious mandala (circular) painting. A simple salad that is aesthetically pleasing too.

In 2 separate bowls, combine the cucumber with the sesame seeds and vinegar, and the beetroot with the mint and oil.

Season to taste and arrange on a serving plate with the beetroot in the centre and the cucumber arranged around it.

Sprinkle the pomegranate seeds over the cucumber and serve.

2 cups cucumber, grated
1 tbsp sesame seeds
2 tbsp white balsamic vinegar
2 cups beetroot, grated
1 tbsp mint, chopped
2 tbsp olive oil
80 g pomegranate seeds
salt and pepper to taste

marvellously muddled

brinjal and tomato salad with smoked paprika vinaigrette

(serves 4 to 6)

Baby brinjals are best for this dish. Blanch the broccoli florets in boiling water to enhance their vibrant green colour and then rinse in cold water. Take care not to overcook the vegetables to preserve their shape and texture.

Heat the olive oil in a pan.

Sauté the onion, add the brinjal and cook for 8 to 10 minutes until tender.

Add the tomatoes and broccoli and toss with the combined dressing ingredients.

Serve on a bed of mixed salad leaves.

olive oil
1 red onion, quartered
8 baby brinjals, slit partially into four
1 punnet cherry tomatoes
2 cups broccoli florets, blanched
mixed salad leaves

dressing
60 ml olive oil
1 tbsp garlic, mashed
½ tsp smoked paprika
30 ml lemon juice
10 ml fresh herbs to taste
salt and pepper to taste

to thai for

asian salad

A riot of colour and texture, combined with a sweet-and-sour dressing, makes this salad good enough to eat on its own. Add the dressing just before serving to preserve the crunchiness of the other ingredients.

Whisk the dressing ingredients together. Combine the salad ingredients.
Pour the dressing over the salad. Mix lightly and garnish with fresh coriander and roasted cashew nuts.

(serves 6)

3 cups red cabbage, finely shredded
2 cups baby cabbage, finely shredded
4 carrots, grated
1 punnet mange tout, blanched and
   sliced into thin strips
1 bunch spring onions, sliced
2 cups lettuce, shredded
1 green chilli, finely chopped (optional)
fresh coriander and roasted cashew nuts
   to garnish

dressing
125 ml vegetable oil
30 ml soya sauce
5 ml sesame oil
75 ml rice vinegar
15 ml lime juice
10 ml sugar
salt and white pepper

43

Bells at Meal Time

the dishes rest in rows
on a hot plate mat.
they line the counter
like inverted bells.
aroma chimes from them
curling incense
into Ixopo air.

our senses sit in silence
before this tinkling.
we open our mouths
to receive the gift
of each grown, cared for,
picked, cooked wonder.
as we balance these tastes
on our tongues,
the pealing begins inside.
(DH)

dudu's moroccan couscous

couscous with nuts, figs and dates

(serves 6 to 8)

This was the very first dish I ever prepared in the BRC kitchen. With Dudu reassuringly at my side, we managed to concoct this hugely popular dish from ingredients we happened to have available on that day. It has featured on the menu almost every week since. It works well as a salad or an accompaniment, but is equally satisfying served as a light summer meal on its own or with a generous dollop of tzatziki.

Soak the couscous in boiling water and cook according to instructions. Fluff with a fork and allow to cool, uncovered.

Combine the almonds, parsley, chickpeas, peppers, dates, figs and onion in a mixing bowl.

Add the couscous and mix together, using a fork until light and fluffy.

Combine all the dressing ingredients and pour over the couscous.

Mix again with a fork. Adjust the seasoning and serve at room temperature.

1 500 g box couscous
1 cup flaked almonds, toasted
1 cup parsley, finely chopped
1 cup cooked chickpeas
1 cup peppers, chopped (try using red, green and yellow, mixed)
¼ cup dates, finely chopped
¼ cup dried figs, finely chopped
½ red onion, finely chopped

dressing
100 ml olive oil
50 ml apple cider vinegar
¼ tsp cinnamon powder
1 small clove garlic, mashed
salt and pepper to taste

45

Tip/variation
It is better to slightly undercook the couscous than overcook it. It will continue to swell even once it is cooling. Overcooked couscous becomes extremely sticky and porridge-like.
For a gluten-free alternative, replace the couscous with 3 cups of cooked quinoa.

'listen to the roofdrops'
says louis
then the rain stops
and the evening drips to stillness
(SC)

tokyo ribbons

marinated wakame and cucumber salad

(serves 6)

This is one of my all-time favourite foods that is a perfect springtime delicacy as the weather starts to warm and the body is cleansed for summer. Rich in minerals, wakame is a subtly flavoured seaweed that is synonymous with Japanese cuisine. It is known most widely as the vegetable ingredient found in bowls of miso soup, but can be used in any number of ways – particularly as a salad ingredient. Wakame is available at most Asian supermarkets. It stores well in a sealed glass container and can be enjoyed in its dried form as a delicious savoury snack.

Rinse the wakame and soak in ice cold water for 15 minutes.

Peel the cucumber and slice into ribbons with a potato peeler, discarding the seeds.

Drain the seaweed and rinse well under cold water. Remove the thick "rib" if desired and slice into smaller strips. (This is usually not necessary if using shredded wakame.)

Combine the marinade ingredients to make a dressing.

Add the marinade to the seaweed and refrigerate for at least 20 to 30 minutes before serving.

Combine the seaweed with the cucumber and the marinade, and sprinkle with sesame seeds.

Serve as an accompaniment or starter with sliced lemon, or as an ingredient for a mixed salad.

8 strips wakame seaweed (or ½ cup shredded dry wakame)
1 cucumber, sliced into ribbons
15 ml sesame seeds (black and brown mixed), to garnish

marinade
100 ml lemon juice
100 ml rice vinegar
20 ml soya sauce
5 ml honey

lungi's sunburst spectacular

mixed salad with edible flowers and sprouts

This section on salads would not be complete without mentioning Lungi, who has an incredible eye for detail. It is easy to spot a salad that has been created by her as she loves arranging the ingredients in colourful combinations and delicate, concentric circles. This luscious summery salad combines edible flowers from our vegetable garden and sprouts tended to daily by the kitchen staff. Sprouting is really so easy and ensures that you always have fresh salad ingredients at hand. If you are able to plant vegetables of your own, it is well worth looking out for edible flower seed mixes, which transform any salad into a visual delight. To preserve the delicate flavours of this salad, dress with the lightest drizzle of quality olive oil and a squeeze of fresh lime juice.

200 g mixed salad leaves (lettuce, rocket, watercress etc)
1 cup fresh basil leaves
1 cup mixed peppers, finely sliced
1 cup cherry tomatoes, halved
olive oil
lime juice
salt and pepper to taste
2 cups alfalfa sprouts
1 cup edible flowers (nasturtium, borage, heartsease pansy, clove-pinks etc)

Combine the salad leaves with the basil, peppers and tomatoes. Dress lightly with olive oil, lime juice and salt and pepper to taste.

Work small handfuls of alfalfa sprouts into balls and arrange on top of the salad.

Arrange flowers in between clusters of alfalfa and serve.

49

Tips for sprouting

Many sophisticated sprouters are available commercially, but we use and recommend the simplest of methods which involves an empty jar, some "mosquito" netting (available at any haberdashery) and an elastic band. Place seeds in the jar, cover the top with the netting and secure in place with the elastic band. It is a great way to re-cycle empty glass and allows you to grow sprouts really easily.

Soak beans/seeds for 8 hours in tepid water to kick-start sprouting, and then drain.
Keep away from direct sunlight.
Rinse well, twice a day and drain.
Depending on the weather, sprouts are ready in 4 to 7 days.
Once sprouted, keep sealed in the fridge and rinse every 2 to 3 days.
To increase the chlorophyll content of alfalfa sprouts, leave for a few hours in the sun once sprouted.
Just one or two tablespoons of alfalfa seeds will produce a jarful of sprouts, but also try sprouting lentils, chickpeas and any kind of bean (except kidney beans, which produce toxic sprouts).

the green machine

green salad with creamy avocado and celery dressing

(serves 6)

A celebration of delightful spring greens complemented by a rich avocado dressing – balancing the lightness of the main ingredients to make a reassuringly cleansing and yet scrumptious feast. The quantities for the salad leaves are approximate, so experiment with different proportions according to what is available. The mung bean sprouts are available at most supermarkets or Asian food markets; choose sprouts that look firm and plump, without any signs of discolouration or browning.

Steam the asparagus for 1 to 2 minutes, until just tender and plunge into cold water.

Trim the tops from the asparagus and keep aside for garnishing. Slice the remaining stems and combine with the baby spinach and watercress in a large serving bowl.

For the dressing, place all the ingredients, except the oil and mint, into a blender. Turn the blender on and gradually add the oil until a thick dressing is formed. Adjust the seasoning and add the mint just before serving.

Combine enough dressing with the mixed leaves, until lightly coated. Garnish with asparagus tips and bean sprouts, and dollops of extra dressing.

100 g asparagus
100 g baby spinach
100 g watercress
1 cup "giant" mung bean
   sprouts, rinsed

dressing
1 avocado
1 tbsp rice vinegar
juice of one lemon
½ cup celery, finely chopped
1 clove garlic
½ cup olive oil (approx.)
½ tsp salt
pepper to taste
1 tbsp mint, chopped

50

monk's robe salad

beetroot and carrot salad

(serves 4 to 6)

1 cup carrot, grated
1 cup alfalfa sprouts, rinsed
juice of 1 orange
1 tbsp sesame seeds, toasted
salt and pepper to taste
1 cup beetroot, grated

Sometimes the simplest of ingredients combined in the most uncomplicated way can produce something that is altogether greater than the sum of its parts. This is one such dish. On a number of occasions, we have been asked for this recipe only to be met with a look of disbelief at the simplicity of the ingredients. But here it is – exactly as it is prepared in the kitchen at the BRC. The deep red and vibrant orange of this salad remind me of the saffron robes worn by the Tibetan monks and nuns.

Using a fork, combine all the ingredients, except the beetroot, in a large mixing bowl.

Once ingredients are combined, gently work in the grated beetroot with a fork.

Serve with *baked potatoes* and *greek-style yoghurt 'n chives*.

Tip/variation
The beetroot is added last so that the different colours are visible in the finished salad.
If alfalfa is not available, replace with 1 cup of grated cucumber.

mains

Sewing Robes at a Retreat Centre

we in a place of quiet
enter this meditation shell.
as breath and blood beat
and bubble in slow time,
we sit clothed in robes
in yellow morning light
still as seeds in granadilla pulp.

we don these mantles
in memory of monks
who gathered rags off corpses
lining the holy rivers.
they stitched a patchwork
to enfold their minding.
they crushed the crocus
to dye the garment
in saffron shades.

in the studio between sittings
we sew scraps of tales –
memory strips frayed at edge,
off-cuts from monsters,
seams of dreams,
patterns of river, reed,
dappled sun and the rain
that whipped our shoulders.
catch all these threads.

as hands guide needles,
patches whisper their
wish to lie together
along hip, chest, elbow, leg.
we slip heads through the neck.
and wrap bodies in this cloth.
hemmed, made whole,
dyed in the seasons' shades
of passion flower nights and days,
we wear our story robes
over wrinkled skin.
(DH)

up to the elbows

macaroni cheese

Take a classic dish and add a little sparkle. Transform it into
something distinctive and luxurious.

Pre-heat the oven to 180°C.

Cook the macaroni in plenty of salted boiling water until just
tender.

Sauté the onion in a little cooking oil until tender. Add the garlic,
mushrooms and herbs and cook for a further 5 minutes, stirring
occasionally. Add the tomato and green pepper. Adjust the
seasoning and set aside.

To make the white sauce, melt the butter in a large saucepan on
a low heat. Stir in the flour until well combined with the butter.
Gradually add the milk, stirring continuously (use a balloon whisk
if the sauce becomes lumpy). Once all the milk has been added,
gradually bring to the boil, stirring until the sauce is thick. Season
with salt, white pepper and a pinch of nutmeg.

Combine the macaroni with the vegetables. Mix in the white sauce
and place in an oven-proof dish. Top with grated cheese and bake
for 30 minutes until the cheese has melted and is lightly flecked.
Allow to stand for a few minutes before serving.

(serves 6)

250 g macaroni
15 ml vegetable oil
1 onion, chopped
1 garlic clove, chopped
150 g mushrooms, sliced
½ tbsp thyme, chopped
½ tbsp marjoram, chopped
1 tomato, chopped
1 small green pepper, chopped
1 cup cheddar cheese, grated

white sauce
50 g butter
50 ml flour
625 ml milk (2½ cups)
salt and white pepper
nutmeg

55

humble beginnings

quinoa rissoles with spinach and chickpeas

Many of the dishes prepared at the Centre are permutations of other dishes that have gradually been tweaked every time they are prepared, until they are so far removed from the original it is difficult to remember where or how they started. This is one such dish that always seemed to have a master-plan entirely of its own. Quinoa lends a delicious, nutty flavour and complements the textures of the other ingredients perfectly. Rich in protein, these vegan rissoles are testament to the fact that vegetarian food need not be laden with dairy to pack a nutritional punch.

Cook the quinoa in 2 cups of water on low heat for approximately 20 minutes. It should be tender but fluffy (do not overcook).

Grease a baking sheet and preheat the oven to 180°C.

In a large saucepan heat the oil and stir-fry the cumin and coriander seeds until lightly browned. Add the onion and thyme and sauté until translucent. Add the spinach and garlic and cook uncovered until tender and the moisture has evaporated.

Place the chickpeas in a large mixing bowl and mash lightly. Add the spinach mixture, quinoa, lemon juice and the seasoning. Add the gram flour and combine the ingredients until the mixture can be shaped into balls. Pour the sesame seeds into a soup bowl or small plate.

Shape into balls just smaller than a tennis ball and roll gently in the sesame seeds. Arrange on a greased baking sheet.

Bake for 20 to 30 minutes until golden and the sesame begins to brown.

Serve with *roasted pepper harissa* and/or *mango and apple chutney*.

1 cup quinoa, rinsed
2 cups water
oil for frying
1 tsp cumin seeds
1 tsp coriander seeds, crushed
1 onion, chopped
 sprig fresh thyme
1 bunch spinach, shredded
1 clove garlic, mashed
1 cup chickpeas, cooked
15 ml lemon juice
1 tsp mixed spice
salt and pepper to taste
¼ cup gram (chickpea) flour
sesame seeds

Tips

Quinoa (pronounced keen-wah) is a small round grain of South American origin that is a welcome addition to the vegetarian kitchen. Not only extremely high in protein and minerals, it is also gluten-free and extremely easy to digest. It is available from most health shops, but can easily be replaced with rice or millet.

The secret to cooking perfect quinoa is to bring it to the boil and then reduce the heat and let it simmer gently until cooked, **without** stirring.

Gram (chickpea) flour is available from Asian supermarkets and most health shops. It is an excellent binding agent that can be used instead of eggs or cheese. Mixed with water, it makes excellent batter which can be seasoned with a little salt and any number of spices.

carrying the moon with fingers

spring rolls

(serves 4 to 6)

The title of this recipe is inspired by the intriguing names given to many Chi Kung exercises. Creating these mouth-watering rolls with rice paper reminds one of the delicate and repetitive Chi Kung movements, and that what we do in the kitchen is intimately entwined with our spiritual practice. Working with the circular sheets of rice paper requires gentleness and poise, and is a perfect way of transforming your kitchen into a sacred space. Purchase the rice sheets from your local Asian supermarket.

Combine all the filling ingredients. Combine all the dressing ingredients. Mix both together.

Place hot water in a large round saucepan or pan. Place 1 rice sheet at a time into the water and allow to hydrate for 1 to 2 minutes until translucent.

Place each sheet on a board covered with a clean dish towel and pat dry. Spoon 3 to 4 tablespoons of the filling in the centre of the sheet and roll into a spring roll, tucking in the sides.

Place on a serving dish and cover with cling film, if not serving immediately.

Serve with *basil tofu mayonnaise*.

8-10 rice paper sheets

filling

1 cup carrot, grated
1 cup red cabbage, grated
50 g mange tout, blanched and thinly sliced
1 cup alfalfa sprouts, rinsed
1 cup chickpea sprouts, rinsed
1 tbsp sesame seeds
1 spring onion, chopped
1 green chilli, finely chopped (optional)

dressing

1 tbsp oil
1 tbsp rice vinegar
1 tbsp lemon/lime juice
1 tsp sesame oil
1 tbsp soya sauce

Tips

It helps to get a little production line going with these spring rolls, keeping all equipment close at hand. Mix together the filling ingredients, then soak your first sheet of rice paper. Once you have placed the first sheet on the dish towel to dry, place the next sheet into the water so that it can hydrate while you are working with the filling. The rolling is complete in no time at all.

See the notes on sprouting in the salad section. Chickpeas are easy to sprout, but are easily replaced with any other sprouts available.

Eating from the Bowl

the monks walked their rough
sandals
door to door in the morning,
unwrapping their begging bowls
from the belly of their robes.

from each hut the aroma
floated its incense from pots.
they received their portion
of roti, masala, nan, tikka,
rice the saffron of their cloth,
a scattering of pecan nuts, mint,
yoghurt, three cherries on a stalk.

when they shared beneath a tree,
robes spread like a table cloth,
did they mish-mash this food
into an all-together taste?
or divide it into sour, salt,
bitter sweet and spice?

their fingers circled in a spiral
from centre to circumference
or rim to hub, tasting inwards,
savouring in each grain and shade
the four corners of their world.
(DH)

gogo fra's phyllo fantasy

mushroom, nut and spinach strudel

Francisca has been a housekeeper at the Centre since 1997. When she first tasted this strudel she declared that she had made a mistake in not becoming part of the kitchen staff earlier in her career. Had she done so, she would have ensured that this strudel was made every day. Although we were not able to turn back time, the least we could do was to make a special strudel just for gogo (grandmother) whenever this dish was prepared.

Sweat the spinach in a saucepan. Set aside in a sieve to drain the liquid. Press lightly with a wooden spoon to remove any excess moisture.

Heat the oil in a large frying pan. Sauté the mushrooms and the onions until all the moisture has evaporated, and the mushrooms are well browned. Add a generous pinch of ground coriander to the mixture while frying to bring out the flavour.

Allow the mushrooms to cool slightly before combining with the chopped nuts and drained spinach. Season with ground nutmeg and salt and pepper to taste. Add the egg and mix well.

Start with one sheet of pastry on a baking tray. Brush with melted butter and cover with another sheet of pastry. Brush with melted butter. Repeat until all layers have been buttered.

Spoon the mixture lengthways onto the pastry (starting approximately 2 cm from the edge closest to you), and roll up, making sure to fold in the edges. Brush the strudel with butter and sprinkle generously with sesame seeds.

Bake at 180°C for 20 to 25 minutes until golden brown.

Slice with a very sharp knife into portions.

½ bunch spinach, veined and
   shredded
oil for frying
2 punnets mushrooms, sliced
2 onions, finely chopped
pinch of ground coriander
1 cup nuts, chopped (pecans
   and almonds work well)
½ tsp ground nutmeg
salt and pepper to taste
1 egg, lightly beaten
8 sheets phyllo pastry
50 g butter, (approx.) melted
sesame seeds

61

Tips/variations

Serving an entire strudel and allowing guests to cut their own portions makes for far more dramatic dining; (we soon learnt that the strudel is so tempting you may find there is none left before everyone gets a taste). The recipe works equally well in individual portions. Butter one sheet of pastry at a time and fill with 3 to 4 heaped tablespoons of mixture. Roll, brush and decorate in the same way. Be sure to wipe the mushrooms clean instead of washing them. Washed mushrooms will release retained moisture and shrink excessively while cooking. Use olive oil instead of butter to brush the pastry for a lighter strudel.

ashoka's wheel

millet and corn tortilla

(serves 8)

A light, but satisfying summer meal, which is best enjoyed with a selection of interesting condiments and a simple salad. Ashoka was a powerful 3rd century king who converted to Buddhism. His regal symbol is a 24-spoked wheel which has been incorporated into the national flag of India. It represents the 24 ennobling human virtues as taught by the Buddha and which Ashoka actively promoted during his reign. Do not worry if you cannot cut one cake into 24 equal slices. This recipe is easily doubled to make two tortillas so that you can cut each one into 12 pieces, thereby keeping the sentiment perfectly intact!

Pre-heat the oven to 200°C and grease a round baking pan.

Rinse the millet and place in a pot with the water. Bring to the boil and then reduce to the lowest heat. Simmer gently for approximately 20 minutes until all the water has been absorbed and the millet is just cooked. Do not stir. Add the butter to the mixture and allow to stand covered for 10 minutes.

While the millet is cooking, heat a little olive oil in a pan. Add the cumin seeds and brown. Add the onion and sauté for 5 minutes.

Mix in the corn, garlic, paprika, peppers and parsley and sauté until the corn is just cooked. Season to taste and allow to cool.

Combine the mixture with the millet, once cool, and adjust the seasoning before adding the eggs and milk.

Mix all the ingredients to form a thick batter.

Spoon into a greased baking tin and bake for 20 to 30 minutes until lightly golden.

Allow to cool slightly in the baking tin before turning out onto a plate or cooling rack. Cut into slices.

Serve with *pumpkin seed and parsley salsa* and *sweet tomato sauce*.

1 cup millet
2 cups water
50 g butter
olive oil
1 tsp cumin seeds
1 red onion, chopped
1 cup frozen corn (mealies)
1 clove garlic, mashed
pinch of smoked paprika
    (optional)
½ green pepper, chopped
½ red pepper, chopped
½ cup parsley, chopped
salt and pepper to taste
3 eggs, lightly beaten
4 tbsp milk

green tara curry

thai green curry paste

For an authentic Thai flavour, nothing beats making your own curry paste from scratch. Search your local Asian supermarket for some of the more exotic ingredients – all are thankfully available in one form or another and are well worth hunting down. Also, check how hot the chillies are before making the paste. If in doubt, rather add fewer chillies and then add more when cooking the actual curry. It is easier to add fire to the curry than take it away.

paste

Place all the ingredients, except the fresh coriander, in a blender. Blend until a thick paste is formed, adding the vegetable oil,
1 tablespoon at a time, until the desired consistency is reached.

Roughly chop the coriander and add to the paste. Blend until a green paste is formed. Do not "over-blend" at this stage as this will destroy the flavour of the coriander.

Place immediately in an airtight container and store in the refrigerator for at least 4 hours before use (overnight is best).
Will keep for up to 3 weeks.

curry

Heat a small amount of oil in a saucepan or wok. Stir-fry the onion for a minute. Add the curry paste and fry for another minute. Add the remaining ingredients and heat through until the broccoli is just tender. Adjust the seasoning and garnish liberally with coriander or basil.

Serve with basmati rice.

Tip

Experiment with different vegetables, and gradually add more curry paste until the spice is just right. As a rule, the potatoes are par-boiled for the curry so that all the ingredients cook for a shorter time to preserve the delicate flavour of the curry paste, and the vegetables retain their crunch.

paste

6 green chillies
6 cloves garlic
3-4 lemon grass stalks, roughly chopped
½ cup dried lime leaves
1 small onion
150 g fresh coriander (rinse well and use whole bunch, roots 'n all)
¼ cup fresh ginger, roughly chopped
1 tbsp coriander seeds
1 tsp peppercorns
1 tsp galangal powder
1 tsp salt
juice of 1 lime
vegetable oil

curry

15 ml oil for frying
1 onion, roughly chopped
3-4 tbsp green curry paste
2 potatoes, cubed and par-boiled until just tender, but still whole
1 green pepper, cubed
1 red pepper, cubed
1 cup baby sweetcorn, diced
1 cup peas, rinsed
2 cups broccoli florets
1 tin coconut cream
salt and pepper to taste
thai basil leaves or coriander leaves to garnish

Chi Kung

you stand grounded,
loose-legged.
scenes of Chinese parks
and a thousand pictograms
rise in your eyes.
we sway, trees in a breeze
to find the centre force
in taproot, bark, sap and branch.
arms flap like prayer flags,
wrapping us in wind.
we slap slack-limbed the body
to wake the cells
from misty sleep.
tap kidneys to chi them.
stretch toes and arch backs.
then we raise and drop arms,
a child on a swing , higher, wilder
above the hills at this retreat
down to the fulcrum forest of knees.
we elongate foot to root
to hot rock, fingers to tree top
to eagle's path, Buddha sky.
we soar with you, winged beings,
landing lightly on trees.
pull the elasticity of the world
between fore and thumb.
we slip back to earth.
become the sunflower at rest
rising to follow the gold
folding to greet the light.
the force new formed flows
along meridians and love lines
beneath our fingers.
skin flower fresh
we belong to this now day.
(DH)

francisco's high-five

falafel

Falafel is a mouth-watering Middle-Eastern dish. These miniature "billiard balls" of taste remind me of David Francisco, a former staff member. David used to make billiard tables. This is a delicate, exacting craft. But at the BRC, you would see him pulling apart a lawn-mower or water-proofing a roof one moment, and making a cosy log fire in the studio or teaching Chi Kung, the next. He was always warm, gracious and friendly, extending his hand for a quick "high- five" to get you through the day. This is David's favourite dish. Like his personality, it combines delicacy with robustness. It is my "high- five" back to him.

Soak the beans in boiling water for at least half an hour. (If using chickpeas or any other beans, soak for at least 8 hours until completely hydrated.)

Place the onion, garlic and fresh herbs in a food processor and blend until very finely chopped (be careful not to over-blend as it will form a very wet paste). Set aside in a bowl.

Place the raw beans in a food processor and blend until they resemble breadcrumbs. The beans must be finely chopped.

Add the beans to the onion mixture and mix in the rest of the seasoning and bicarbonate of soda. Stir together and slowly add the gram flour until the mixture can be rolled into balls (sometimes the mixture will have more liquid; just keep adding flour a little at a time until it sticks together).

Shape approximately 1 tablespoon of the mixture into a ball and place on a tray or baking sheet. Repeat with the rest of the mixture.

Heat 3 cm of oil in a saucepan or small pot. Once the oil is hot, carefully drop the balls into the oil, about 6 at a time. (If they stick to the bottom, the oil is not hot enough.)

Fry until the outside is dark brown and crispy. Drain on kitchen paper.

Serve with warm pita bread and a selection of fillings such as *tzatziki, tarka hummus, harissa,* shredded lettuce and red cabbage. Make up your own perfect combinations.

1 cup black-eyed beans
1 large onion, peeled and
   roughly chopped
6 cloves garlic, peeled
1 cup parsley, roughly chopped
½ cup coriander leaves, roughly
   chopped
1 tbsp ground cumin
2 tsp ground coriander
1 tsp salt
pepper to taste
½ tsp bicarbonate of soda
3 tbsp gram (chickpea) flour
oil for deep frying

67

Tip
Although traditionally made with chickpeas, I found that black-eyed beans soaked much more quickly and were ready in less than an hour as opposed to soaking chickpeas overnight.

more is more, dhal

spicy mixed lentils with coconut

(serves 6 to 8)

Dhal (split lentil) is a good stand-by dish that is well worth adding to your culinary repertoire. It makes an affordable and nutritious accompaniment to any curry and is equally good served on its own with a flat bread or brown rice. The recipe is easily increased with the addition of more water – perfect for days when you need to adjust quantities for unexpected guests. Buy a mixture of dhals and mix them in a large tub or jar ready for use. Try any combination of moong, chana, oil, toor and whole moong from the seemingly endless variety available at Asian supermarkets. Most dhals are quite watery and I prefer a thicker dhal. If you are not sure, start with a smaller amount of water and keep adding a little at a time until you reach a consistency you like. Leftover dhal refrigerated overnight makes a delicious paté.

2 tbsp sunflower oil
1 tbsp cumin seeds
2 tsp mustard seeds
3-4 whole cardamom
1 large onion, chopped
1 stalk celery, finely chopped
2 tbsp grated ginger
½ cup roughly chopped fresh
   coriander
2 tomatoes, chopped
1 tin coconut milk
2 cups mixed dhal
salt and pepper to taste

dried spices – 1 tsp of each of
the following:
cumin
medium curry
ground coriander
turmeric
garam masala (added at the
   end)
fresh coriander to garnish

Heat the oil in a large pot with the cumin and mustard seeds and the cardamom until the mustard seeds start to pop.

Add the onion and celery and sauté until tender (about 5 minutes).

Add the ginger and 2 tablespoons of the fresh coriander. Fry for another minute.

Add the tomato and all dried spices (except the garam masala) and continue to sauté on a medium heat until the tomato is soft.

Add the coconut milk and dhal and enough water to cover the dhal twice over. Bring to the boil and then reduce the heat to simmer for up to one hour. Do not add salt for the first 20 minutes of cooking.

Stir from time to time. Once the dhal is cooked, adjust the seasoning; add the garam masala and chopped coriander before serving.

Serve with *potato and spinach with cumin* and *spinach and carrot bhajias.*

69

sunday's treasure

vegetable curry

We serve this hearty vegetable curry with an assortment of side dishes or "sambals", adorned with flowers from our garden. Curry is a satisfying dish to master as it bears the unmistakable signature of its creator. Spices are temperamental ingredients to work with because they vary so greatly in intensity, depending on their freshness and quality. The quantities in this recipe are therefore a guide only. Experiment!

Pour a liberal amount of cooking oil in a pot and add the spice seeds, cinnamon, star aniseed and bay leaf. Stir for one minute and then add the onion. Fry for up to 10 minutes until the onion is translucent and golden, reducing the heat if necessary.

Add the coconut, ginger, garlic and coriander. Stir for a minute. Mix in the ground spices and fry for a further minute. Gradually add the tomato and cook until it is tender.

Add the potatoes and carrots and cover with water (this is usually all the liquid needed). Season liberally with salt and white pepper.

Gradually add the rest of the vegetables and ensure that they are still firm when serving.

When the potatoes and carrots are cooked, the curry is ready to be served. Adjust the seasoning and stir in the chopped coriander.

Serve with basmati rice, *spinach and carrot bhajias* or *samoosas* and a selection of sambals.

(serves 6)

60 ml vegetable oil for frying
5 ml each of the seeds: mustard, cumin, coriander, fennel, cardamom
1 stick cinnamon
1 star aniseed
1 bay leaf
2 onions, chopped
½ cup desiccated coconut
¼ cup ginger, grated
¼ cup garlic, grated
½ cup fresh coriander, chopped
15 ml each of the ground spices: cumin, coriander and curry powder
4 tomatoes (the ripest you can find, chopped)
6 cups cubed vegetables (potato, carrot, baby corn, butternut, broccoli, peas etc)
salt and white pepper
½ cup fresh coriander, chopped (to serve)

A treasury of sambals

chop 2 onions, 1 fresh tomato; combine with 1 grated carrot and chopped coriander
combine chopped cucumber, tomato, green pepper and chopped coriander
toast ½ cup of desiccated coconut and ½ cup of sunflower seeds; combine
combine 1 cup yoghurt with ½ teaspoon turmeric and 1 tablespoon chopped mint
apple and mango chutney
brinjal atchaar
chopped green chillies
sliced banana

chakra-laka

traditional south african chakalaka

(serves 4 to 6)

Simple baked beans get dressed up in this versatile dish which can often be found at our lunch table smothering baked potatoes hot out of the oven. Works equally well with rice or with the more traditional putu (maize meal).

Heat the vegetable oil in a large saucepan. Add the coriander seeds, onion and chilli, and sauté for 5 minutes until the onion is translucent.

Add the garlic, tomato, celery, carrot and green pepper and cook over a medium heat for a further 5 minutes, stirring to prevent sticking.

Add the paprika, curry powder and chopped parsley and combine with the onion mixture.

Add the baked beans and kidney beans to the mixture. Reduce the heat and simmer gently for 20 minutes, stirring occasionally until the carrots are cooked, but still firm. Add a little water if the mixture is becoming too dry or sticking to the bottom of the pan.

Adjust the seasoning and serve.

15 ml vegetable oil
1 tsp coriander seeds (optional)
1 large onion, chopped
1 green chilli, whole
2-3 cloves garlic, crushed
1 large tomato, chopped
2 stalks celery, finely chopped
2 cups grated carrot
1 green pepper, seeded and
 chopped
1 tsp paprika
1 tsp medium curry powder
2 tbsp parsley or coriander, finely
 chopped
1 tin baked beans
1 cup cooked kidney beans or 1
 tin beans, rinsed and drained
salt and pepper to taste

Tips
Add a whole chilli to stews and sauces; you can then taste how hot the dish is becoming while it is cooking and take out the chilli when it is just right.

If using tinned kidney beans, add them after the mixture has cooked for 10 minutes, otherwise they tend to disintegrate during the cooking.

lindi's lasagne layers

brinjal lasagne

(serves 6 to 8)

Lasagne is one of the most satisfying comfort foods in the world. There are many ways of making this dish, but this is our favourite version. Although deceptively simple, the addition of sliced brinjal makes it special.

Sauté the onion in olive oil for 15 to 20 minutes until caramelised and golden. Reduce the heat if the onion starts to brown. Add fresh marjoram and stir for another minute before adding the tomato. Add salt and simmer covered for up to 2 hours until thick and rich in flavour.

Allow the brinjal to stand, salted, for 20 to 30 minutes. Rinse well and pat dry using a clean tea towel. Either brush lightly with olive oil and bake at 200°C (approximately 20 minutes, turning half way through), or shallow fry in oil until golden. Drain well between sheets of kitchen paper.

To make the white sauce, melt the butter in a large saucepan on a low heat. Stir in the flour until completely combined with the butter. Gradually add the milk, stirring continuously (use a balloon whisk if the sauce becomes lumpy). Once all the milk has been added, gradually bring to the boil, stirring until the sauce is thick. Season with salt, white pepper and a pinch of nutmeg. Reduce the heat if the sauce is catching at the bottom of the saucepan – this will prevent burning.

Pre-heat the oven to 200°C. Line the bottom of a large oven-proof dish with a thin layer of tomato sauce, followed by a layer of lasagne sheets. Place a layer of brinjal on the sheets and top with a layer of white sauce and a little cheese. Repeat with another layer of pasta and brinjal, but this time top with a layer of tomato sauce (omit the cheese). Repeat in this fashion until 3 to 4 layers have been created. After adding each layer of pasta, press down gently to ensure that the layers are even.

Finish with a layer of the remaining white sauce, and top with the remaining cheese. Place the dish in the oven and bake until the cheese is melted and lightly browned. Remove from the oven and allow to stand for 10 minutes before serving.

15 ml olive oil
1 onion, finely chopped
1 sprig marjoram, rinsed
4 x 400 g tins Italian tomatoes, chopped
2 kg brinjal, sliced and salted
salt and pepper to taste
2 cups mozzarella cheese, grated
12-15 lasagne sheets

white sauce
125 g butter
250 ml flour
1¼ litres milk (5 cups)
salt and white pepper
nutmeg

Variations
Use any combination of cooked vegetables for the filling; approximately one cup of filling for each layer. To keep the lasagne simple, replace the brinjal with cooked and well-drained spinach.

beatrice's butternut bake

our famous butternut and feta pie

This is one of those dishes that was created in the kitchen with ingredients that were available at the time. On a day that we were due to make our spinach and feta bake, there was a shortage of spinach, so Beatrice and I decided instead to adapt the recipe and use the mountain of butternut we had somehow accumulated in the pantry. The result was an instant hit and has been part of the regular menu ever since. Usually served with spicy tomato couscous and lashings of fresh tzatziki.

Pre-heat the oven to 180°C.

Chop enough butternut to fill an ovenproof dish.

Add the onion, garlic, feta cheese and thyme.

Season with salt, pepper and mixed spice.

Drizzle with olive oil and mix together lightly with a metal spoon until the butternut is coated.

Arrange snugly into the dish and top with the crust mixture. Sprinkle with extra sesame seeds. Bake until the butternut is tender and the crust is golden (approximately 45 minutes).

crust

Blend day-old, wholemeal bread in a food processor for the best breadcrumbs.

Combine all the ingredients with enough olive oil to bind them together lightly. The mixture should form a ball when pressed in the palm of the hand, but crumble just as easily. Too much oil will produce a greasy crust.

1½ kg butternut, peeled and
   cubed
1 red onion, roughly chopped
2 cloves garlic, chopped
400 g feta cheese, cubed
4-5 sprigs thyme
olive oil (approx. ¼ cup)
salt and pepper to taste
mixed spice

crust

2 cups fresh breadcrumbs
1 tomato, chopped
½ cup sesame seeds (plus
   extra to garnish)
1 cup grated cheddar cheese
   (optional)
olive oil

77

Napkins and Guests

in the dining space
the recipe book,
rests on the knees
of the stand,
relaxed in lotus,
open for the day
like Buddha hands
palms raised,
lined with tastes and text.

the saffron napkins
sit beneath the pages,
waiting row on row
like nuns and monks
for guests to take them
with bowls and spoons
to the matching table cloths.

somebody has written our names
lovingly, fleetingly on a sticker
so we can return to this same serviette
these retreat days and nights.

then the napkin,
like the soul,
will find its way
through churning water,
wind and a drying line
back to its posture
folded on the counter,
my name peeled off,
another in its place.
(DH)

over the moon

pasta crescents with nuts, cheese and sage filling

Homemade pasta is truly worth the effort. Investing in a pasta machine not only makes the rolling a little easier, but also allows you to create more adventurous shapes with greater perfection. Any type of nuts can be used for the filling. Depending on your preference, opt for white cheddar for a mild flavour, or a pecorino or parmesan for a richer, more robust taste. Stuffed pasta is best served with the simplest of sauces. Drizzle the crescents with a little olive oil and sprinkle with chopped sage and parmesan.

Dry roast the nuts at 180°C or in a frying pan until lightly toasted. Allow to cool.

Place the nuts in a food processor and pulse blend until coarsely chopped.

Add the remaining ingredients and blend until combined. Set aside.

Roll out the dough. Cut the rolled pasta into round shapes using a biscuit cutter. Place a teaspoon of filling in the middle. Wet the edges with water using a brush. Fold in half and pinch the edges to seal.

Spread the crescents on a floured tea towel and sprinkle with flour or mealie meal. Allow to dry 1 to 2 hours before cooking.

Cook the crescents in boiling salted water for 2 to 3 minutes, stirring occasionally to prevent sticking.

Drain and serve immediately.

pasta
300 g flour
3 eggs
15 ml vegetable oil
5 ml salt

filling
200 g chopped nuts, lightly
    toasted
250 g cream cheese
100 ml grated white cheese
2 cloves garlic, chopped
15 ml chopped sage
salt and pepper to taste

kneading
Divide the dough into 2 pieces. Knead by pushing the dough with the heel of your hand.
Knead until elastic and the dough peels from the work surface in one piece. Repeat with the second half of the dough. Cover with a bowl and stand for 1 hour.

handmade
Sift the flour onto a work surface. Make a well in the centre and add the eggs, oil and salt.
Using your fingertips, working in the centre, mix the eggs, oil and salt before combining with the flour. Gradually mix in the flour to make a firm dough. If sticky, add more flour. Press into a ball, cover and rest.

food processor
Place the flour and salt in the food processor. Add the oil and one egg and pulse for 30 seconds.
Add another egg and pulse a few times to mix. Add the last egg and continue working until the dough is thoroughly mixed. Turn the dough onto a work surface and press into a ball.

rolling
Flour the work surface. Divide into 4 portions. Work with one portion at a time. Cover the remaining dough at all times.
Roll with a rolling pin to the thickness of a card, or use a pasta machine.
Shape the pasta according to recipe.

festival of colours

vegetarian sushi rolls

Sushi is a blessing for creative souls. It allows your kitchen to become a canvas for a riot of colours in endless combinations. Sushi is not limited to fish – once you get the knack of it you will find that the possibilities for vegetarian sushi are limitless. The only daunting thing about sushi is the fact that the rice is extremely sticky and, without careful handling, it will soon cover both hands, making rolling more difficult. A little cooking oil rubbed into your hands before handling the rice will prevent it from sticking and makes rolling a pleasure.

sushi rice

Cook the rice on low heat for 10 to 15 minutes.

Set aside and rest in a covered container for 30 minutes.

Cover a tray with cling film and spread the rice over it.

Combine all ingredients for the vinegar mix. Drizzle this over the rice.

Use a spatula to combine the rice and vinegar mix.

Allow to cool completely.

sushi rolls

Cover the sushi mat with cling film. Place the vegetable oil in a small bowl for dipping your fingers as you work.

Cut the seaweed sheet in half for smaller rolls; leave whole for larger rolls.

Place the seaweed on a rolling mat, shiny side down. Rub a little oil into finger tips and then spread the rice in a thin layer over the seaweed, leaving a 1 cm gap from the edge at the top of the sheet.

Place the various toppings in a line about 3 cm from the bottom of the sheet. Using the rolling mat to guide you, lift and roll the seaweed to cover the toppings. Using the mat, gently pull the seaweed back towards yourself to seal the filling.

Roll the rest of the seaweed to make a sausage-shaped tube. Using a very sharp knife, cut into equal sized portions and serve with soya, wasabi and pickled ginger.

sushi rice
1 cup sushi rice
1½ cups water

vinegar mix
50 ml rice vinegar
25 ml castor sugar
5 ml salt
5 ml mirin
dash lemon juice

sushi rolls
8-10 nori seaweed sheets
wasabi paste
mayonnaise
brown and black sesame
  seeds, lightly toasted
selection of vegetables,
  sliced or shredded
vegetable oil
cling film
sushi mat

Combinations
grated baby marrow with wasabi
  and sesame
grated carrot and alfalfa sprouts
cream cheese and mixed peppers
avocado, cucumber and mayonnaise
grated beetroot and umeboshi
  (sour plum) vinegar
smoked tofu and rocket
sauerkraut and carrot
omelet and mustard cress

81

the good shepherd's pie

hearty lentil and potato winter pie

(serves 8 to 10)

This is a wonderful alternative to the traditional meaty shepherd's pie. It is an enduring favourite at the Centre, especially on cold and misty Ixopo days, served with lightly steamed, seasonal vegetables and a generous helping of caramelised baby onions. Substitute lentils with cooked aduki or kidney beans, and experiment with different combinations of fresh herbs. Strict vegetarians should be sure to buy vegetarian worcestershire sauce as many commercial brands contain fish extracts.

Cover the lentils in boiling water and cook rapidly for 10 minutes. Reduce the heat and simmer until tender, adding more water as needed. Drain and set aside.

Simmer the potatoes in lightly salted water until tender. Drain and place in a large mixing bowl.

Heat the oil in a large saucepan and sauté the onion for 3 to 4 minutes. Add the garlic, ginger, tomato, carrots, pepper and herbs and sauté for a further 5 minutes until the onion is translucent.

Add the lentils and simmer gently for 20 minutes. Add a little water if the mixture becomes too dry. Adjust the seasoning and add the worcestershire sauce.

Combine the butter, cream and parsley with the potatoes and mash until smooth. Add salt and pepper to taste.

Place the lentil mixture at the bottom of a large ovenproof dish. Spoon small quantities of mashed potato onto the lentil mixture. Smooth with a spatula or fork to form a crust over the lentils. Drag a fork lightly over the potato to decorate.

Bake at 180°C for 20 to 30 minutes until golden brown.

Serve with *caramelised baby onions*.

500 g brown lentils, soaked
1 kg potatoes, peeled and cubed
1 tbsp cooking oil
1 large onion, chopped
2-3 cloves garlic, minced
1 tbsp ginger, grated
1 large tomato, chopped
3 carrots, chopped
1 pepper, chopped
1 tsp marjoram, finely chopped
1 tsp thyme, finely chopped
1 tsp worcestershire sauce
1 tbsp butter
½ cup cream or milk
¼ cup parsley, finely chopped

83

beans in a sizzle

vegetable and tofu teriyaki kebabs

The humble soya bean has many guises. For centuries the East has been obsessed with transforming this nutritionally dense, but difficult to digest, bean into food that is not only palatable, but easy on the stomach too. Tofu is made from soya milk in very much the same way that cheeses are made from cow's milk. While it contains little flavour on its own, it eagerly soaks up any flavours it meets on its journey from preparation to the table. In this dish, the tofu is combined with vegetables in a rich teriyaki marinade and then grilled to sticky sweet perfection. Any vegetables can be used, including mushrooms, peppers, shallots, baby corn, cherry tomatoes and marrows. Enjoy as a starter, a main course or as a sizzling vegetarian barbecue.

marinade
65 ml soya sauce
65 ml rice wine or mirin
30 ml brown sugar
30 ml sesame oil
30 ml rice vinegar
2 cloves garlic, pressed
10 ml ginger, grated

skewers
1 block firm tofu, cut into
  cubes
4-5 cups mixed vegetables,
  cut into cubes

85

Mix together the marinade ingredients. Reserve half to use during grilling. Place the remaining half in a plastic bag with the tofu and vegetables.

Marinade for at least one hour, turning occasionally.

Soak bamboo skewers in water for 30 minutes. Thread the tofu and vegetables onto skewers.

Place the skewers in a baking dish and pour over any remaining marinade from the bag.

Grill either on an open fire or under a hot oven grill, or on a grill pan on the stove.

Brush with reserved teriyaki sauce and turn when necessary to ensure that all sides are evenly browned.

Serve with the *asian salad*, noodles or rice.

african flamenco

baked spanish tortilla with madumbis and potato

(serves 6 to 8)

Tortilla or frittata is a baked omelette traditionally made with fried potatoes and onions. Because the potatoes are boiled for this recipe instead of fried, it creates a wonderfully light tortilla that can be enjoyed either hot out the oven or sliced and served cold with a salad. The madumbis add a lovely waxy texture, but if you want to make the more traditional tortilla, simply double the quantity of regular potato.

Pre-heat the oven to 180°C.

Place the potatoes and madumbis in separate pots of boiling water and simmer until cooked. While cooking, prepare the vegetable mixture.

Heat a little oil in a saucepan or wok. Sauté the onion for 8 to 10 minutes. Add the garlic, tomato, chopped herbs (not parsley) and spices, and stir for another 2 minutes.

Add the baby marrows and red pepper and stir-fry until the marrow is just tender. Adjust the seasoning and set aside.

Peel the madumbis once cooked and slice both the madumbis and potatoes.

Arrange half of the madumbi and potato mixture in an oven-proof dish and then spoon over half of the cooked vegetable mixture. Repeat with the remaining mixture.

Beat the eggs, season lightly with salt and pepper. Mix in the chopped parsley.

Pour over the vegetables and spread evenly using a wooden spoon, pressing down gently to set in place. Add extra egg if necessary.

Top with grated cheese, if desired, and bake for approximately 45 minutes until cooked through and golden on top.

Allow to cool before serving.

500 g potatoes, peeled
500 g madumbis, washed
vegetable oil for frying
1 large red onion, chopped
2 garlic cloves, mashed
1 small tomato, chopped
2 tbsp fresh mixed herbs,
   chopped
½ tsp ground cumin
1 tsp ground coriander
1 tsp smoked paprika
250 g baby marrows, thinly
   sliced
1 red pepper, thinly sliced
salt and pepper to taste
6 large eggs
½ cup parsley, finely
   chopped
½ cup cheddar cheese,
   grated (optional)

Variation

For a spinach tortilla, omit the tomato, baby marrow and peppers and add 1 bunch (about 15 leaves) of shredded spinach to the onion. Cook uncovered until the moisture has evaporated and then proceed as normal.

chrisi's quills

spelt penne with tofu, red pepper and arame

(serves 6)

The queen of pasta dishes that is both sophisticated and healthy; a perfect mingling of Eastern and Mediterranean flavours. Spelt is an older strain of wheat that is enjoying much deserved favour as a substitute for high gluten-containing commercial wheats. Its fuller flavour and nutty aroma lend something special to any pasta dish. Arame is often seen as a "beginner's" seaweed, because it has a mild flavour and a delicate texture, and is easily befriended by even the most suspicious of palates. Remember, when using seaweed, to soak in cold water beforehand to rehydrate completely and remove any excess salt.

olive oil
1 onion, chopped
1 red pepper, halved and cored
2 cloves garlic, crushed
1 kg red tomatoes, chopped
¼ cup arame seaweed, soaked in
   ice cold water
500 g spelt penne
400 g smoked tofu, cubed (can
   be shallow fried beforehand –
   optional)
pinch of smoked paprika
1 tbsp fresh coriander, chopped
   (optional)
salt and pepper to taste
½ cup pumpkin seeds, toasted

Sauté the onion in olive oil until translucent. Add the red pepper and garlic and cook for a further minute.

Add the tomatoes and simmer gently for up to one hour until thick and velvety.

Steam the seaweed in a saucepan for 5 minutes and then rinse under cold water. Drain and set aside.

Cook the pasta in plenty of salted water until al dente.

Add the seaweed and tofu to the tomato sauce. Add the paprika, coriander, seasoning and pumpkin seeds just before serving.

Drain the pasta, combine with the sauce and serve immediately.

89

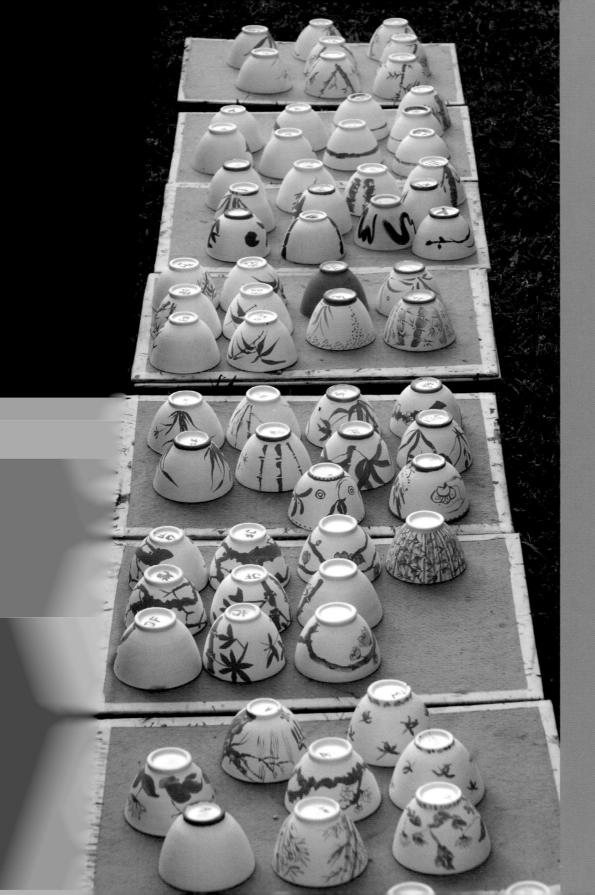

Walking Meditation

the bird calls. we rise
from mat and pad
and follow its path.
robes swish and sway.
a light wind runs along arms.
step in single file,
circle the Buddha who sits
unmoving in the middle,
bird perched on a branch.
round the labyrinth
silent at centre,
we shape an outer ring.
hoop the zen garden
where bird lights on a rock.
wing and feather led, we
loop back to the hall
where we sink onto mats
still as the candle wick.

and all the while, between gongs,
we have sat here not moving
under rain on the roof.
yet we find Buddha.
labyrinth, zen garden
all inside us now
after the imagined
ankle flex, arm swing shuffle
follow of the bird.
(DH)

salt of the earth

baked potatoes

(serves 8)

The humble baked potato is not to be underestimated. Once you are done with the simple task of preparing the potatoes and placing them in the oven, you can get down to the serious business of choosing an assortment of alluring toppings. We usually serve the baked potatoes on a huge platter and then line up a mouth-watering selection of toppings, each more tantalising than the other. Scrub the potatoes before baking to ensure that all potential pesticide residues, which are concentrated in the skin, are removed. By rubbing the spuds in a little olive oil and salt, a deliciously crispy skin is created in the oven while they gently bake to perfection.

Pre-heat the oven to 200°C and grease a baking sheet.

Scrub the potatoes to remove their skins. Place the oil in a small bowl and stir in the salt. Pour a little olive oil in the palm of your hand and rub each potato to coat – much like washing your hands with soap.

Place on a baking sheet in the oven for one hour until cooked through. Test with either a skewer or fork.

8 large baking potatoes
½ cup olive oil (approx.)
1 tsp sea salt

Our typical BRC spread includes:
butter
chakalaka
greek style cream 'n chives
monk's robe salad
guacamole
grated cheese

For something slightly different,
try a combination of:
tarka hummus
red pepper harissa
pumpkin and parsley salsa
alfalfa sprouts

91

spears in a crust

asparagus tart

A big hit at lunch time, served with a simple salad and mixed steamed vegetables. The secret is patience while the filling mixture is cooking. Keep stirring the mixture until it is thick and velvety. Anything less than undivided attention at this stage will prevent the finished product from setting. Bake the quiche until it is lightly browned on the surface. Then switch off the oven and let it settle until cool.

pastry

Pre-heat the oven to 180°C.

Sift the flours and seasoning into a mixing bowl. Reserve the bran from the sifted nutty wheat, and return to the bowl (do not discard).

Add the cheese and butter, and mix well until the dough is formed.

Line an oven-proof serving dish with the pastry, pressing down with your fingers until evenly spread out (be sure to leave no holes).

filling

Melt the butter in saucepan. Add the flour, 1 tablespoon at a time until the mixture forms a thick paste.

Gradually add the liquid while whisking to remove any lumps. Add the eggs and whisk until smooth.

Stir over a low heat until the mixture is the consistency of a thick white sauce. Mix in the grated cheese and heat gently just until the cheese has melted. Season with salt and pepper.

Add half of the asparagus. Pour into the pastry. Add the rest of the asparagus. Bake for 25 to 30 minutes until lightly browned on top. Turn off the heat and let the quiche rest in the oven for 30 minutes. Allow to cool to room temperature for easier cutting.

pastry
2 cups flour (1 cup nutty wheat
    and 1 cup cake flour)
salt and pepper to taste
2 ml paprika
2 ml cayenne pepper
2 ml mustard
2 cups grated cheese
250 ml butter, soft

filling
50 g butter
4 tbsp flour (approx.)
4 cups liquid (made up of
    drained asparagus water
    and milk)
4 jumbo egg yolks (if eggs
    are small, add extra)
2 cups grated cheese
salt and pepper to taste
2 tins asparagus cuts,
    drained and liquid
    reserved

93

Raku: a feast of earth, fire, air and water

The raku retreats at the Centre started when Anthony Shapiro, one of South Africa's renowned master potters, lived and worked at the Centre.

Raku means enjoyment, happiness, elation. And this is indeed the palpable mood during these retreats. The word is associated with the way pottery is fired and treated when it comes out of the kiln. The entire process is delightfully unpredictable because your pot is deliberately subjected to some very rough treatment that causes it to be heated violently, suffocated in sawdust and, still hot, immersed in cold water. This causes the glaze to fuse and craze randomly and the clay to blacken. The effects are largely unpredictable but often quite stunning – what the Japanese call *Shibuie*: Accidental Beauty.

At the retreat, we first learn to make the characteristic sumi-e brush marks used in traditional Chinese and Japanese art. We practise on paper and decorate a number of tea bowls with bamboo, orchid and plum blossom patterns. We then mill around the 40 gallon drum that has been made into a kiln. Anthony inserts the bowls and subjects them to the incredible heat of his blow torch. We then wait to see what has happened to the glaze and our decoration as the bowls emerge from the sawdust and water.

The effects are often stunning. But not all pots survive this ordeal. Some crack, others have their decoration erased. Some retreatants bury their broken bowls in our labyrinth with tears in their eyes …

Raku is like life: sweet-sour.

When the brush dances and the ink sings

I joined a traditional sumi-e (Japanese brush painting) studio in Kyoto, Japan, in the early 1970s. It was run by an elderly teacher who did not speak a word of English. Nor did any of the students with whom I spent the days trying to master this very difficult art form. I therefore just watched and copied how they held and manipulated their brushes.

We were painting the sequence of orchid leaf patterns that are part of the ancient practice of mastering not only the marks we made on paper, but also the blank spaces left between them. This is extraordinarily challenging. There are seven principal leaves to this classic composition, all crossing each other at various angles and curvatures. Each long, thin leaf changes its shape as it bends, twists and turns. One leaf in this composition bends down, its tip pointing to the ground. The teacher and his students tried to tell me something about that tip. I kept doing it wrong.

Then, one day, the teacher came past and asked everyone to have a look. My down-looking leaf had made it! Everyone clapped and laughed. The teacher ran off with my painting, mumbling "Zoffenir, zoffenir". I was puzzled.

A few days later an English-speaking visitor arrived. I asked him what had happened. He explained that the tip of my down-pointing leaf had to show, somehow, that it longed to look at the sky – like the other leaves in the composition. When, at last, my leaf showed this "cloud longing", the teacher had confiscated my painting as a "souvenir".

sides & sauces

great balls of fire

spinach and carrot bhajias

(serves 8)

These "chilli bites" started as a humble addition to the curry served at the Centre. We soon learnt that we were going to have to make a whole lot more to satisfy eager palates. The recipe was doubled, trebled and eventually quadrupled before we finally managed to make enough to accompany the main meal. The secret for its popularity is the combination of ready-made "chilli bite mix" with plain gram (chickpea) flour. Although the "ready mix" does not contain any synthetic ingredients, it tends to be quite salty and intensely fiery. By adding the extra flour, the flavours are softened without having to season the mixture from scratch. It also makes a few extra bhajias; you will need them! When frying the bhajias, it is important to get the temperature just right – if the oil is too cool, the batter will drop to the bottom and stick to the saucepan; if too hot, the bhajias will brown on the outside, but remain raw inside. Adjust the temperature with the first batches and cook only one or two at a time until they emerge perfectly golden and cooked throughout.

Place the dry ingredients, the vegetables, the coriander and ginger in a mixing bowl.

Add enough water to form a stiff batter. Mix well.

Cover the bowl with a damp cloth and let the mixture stand for at least 30 minutes (or refrigerate overnight).

Heat 3 to 4 cm of oil in a pot or deep pan (enough for deep frying).

Stir the mixture and then drop 4 to 6 spoonfuls at a time into hot oil. Fry until golden brown and drain on kitchen paper.

1 500 g box "chilli bite mix"
½ cup gram (chickpea) flour
1-2 carrots, peeled and grated
½ red onion, halved and finely sliced
4 spinach leaves, veined and finely sliced
¼ cup fresh coriander, roughly chopped
1 tsp ginger, grated
1-2 cups water
sunflower oil for frying

Tip

When working with this kind of batter, it is always a good idea to work with two soup spoons. One is used to scoop batter from the bowl, and the other to scrape the batter from the first spoon into the oil. It is a great way to keep your hands clean and minimise the splatter.

tarka hummus

chickpea dip

(serves 4 to 6)

This is our version of the ever-popular classic – with a spicy twist. For this hummus, an Indian tarka is made so that the spices are toasted, imparting a rich and nutty flavour to the chickpeas, while giving the dip a wonderful texture. This recipe makes a thick hummus, so add more lemon juice or oil for a more runny consistency. To add extra bite, keep the chilli aside, and blend with the rest of the mixture.

½ cup olive oil (approx.)
1 tsp cumin seeds
2 tsp garlic, grated
1 green chilli (optional)
1 tsp ground cumin
½ tsp ground coriander
black pepper to taste
1 tbsp tahini paste
3 tbsp fresh lemon juice
2 cups chickpeas, cooked
   (or 1 tin)
½ tsp sea salt
olive oil and cayenne
   pepper

Heat the oil in a small saucepan. Add the cumin seeds. Once they start to brown, add the garlic and chilli. When the garlic starts to brown, add the dried spices (and black pepper) and stir for another minute over a medium heat until lightly browned and aromatic.

Remove from the heat and take out the chilli. Stir in the tahini and then stir in the lemon juice.

Place the chickpeas in a food processor. Add the tarka (fried spice mixture) and blend until smooth. Add the sea salt, and add more liquid if necessary.

Smooth into a serving bowl. Drizzle with olive oil and sprinkle with cayenne pepper.

Serve with the *BRC brown bread*, *pita breads* or *baked potatoes*.

ixopo tzatziki

greek yoghurt and mint dip

A perennial favourite to accompany our vegetable bakes. Essential whenever couscous is served. Fresh mint is best, but can be replaced with dried mint or dill instead.

Squeeze excess moisture from cucumber.

Combine all the ingredients in a bowl. Adjust the seasoning.

Allow to chill for at least 1 hour before serving.

(serves 6)

1 cup grated cucumber
2 cups greek yoghurt
1 clove garlic, mashed
1 tbsp finely chopped mint
   (or dill)
salt and pepper to taste

chibini fire

spicy tomato couscous

(serves 4 to 6)

At the end of summer, the rolling hills of Chibini valley are ablaze with veld-fires that mark the coming of winter. This dish, with its deep reds and fiery spices, is usually served in towering mounds much like those hills of the valley, and is a perfect accompaniment to other hearty dishes when the weather starts to cool.

Sauté the onion in olive oil for 3 to 4 minutes until tender.

Add the garlic and spices and stir for 30 seconds.

Add the chopped tomatoes, pepper and herbs. Add about 2 to 3 cups of water.

Season and simmer for 20 to 30 minutes. Add more water if necessary.

Add the couscous, cover and turn off the heat.

After approximately 2 minutes, stir through with a fork. Let the couscous stand until it is cooked (4 to 5 minutes).

Add salt and pepper to taste.

Serve with *butternut and feta bake* and *tzatziki*.

500 g couscous
1 small onion, chopped
olive oil
1 clove garlic, mashed
½ tsp paprika
¼ tsp ground cumin
¼ tsp ground coriander
¼ tsp ground chilli
   (optional)
1 tin chopped tomatoes
½ red or green pepper,
   chopped
sprig of fresh marjoram
   and thyme
2-3 cups water (approx.)
salt and pepper to taste

try, try, triangle

potato, red onion and sweetcorn samoosas

Samoosa folding is not nearly as technical as it seems. There is a lot to be said for food that is repetitive in its creation. After settling into a rhythm, it becomes soothing and stress-free work. The mantra is "fold diagonally, fold up". Criss-cross the folding until a perfect triangle is formed, enclosing the filling completely. Ready-made samoosa sheets are available at most supermarkets and Asian food stores. They freeze well and are a great kitchen staple to have at hand as they can be rolled up with any number of fillings and cooked within minutes.

Simmer the potatoes in salted water until soft (overcooking is fine).

Heat the oil in a large pot. Add the seeds and heat until the mustard seeds start popping.

Add the onions, salt and turmeric. Fry on a low heat for 20 to 25 minutes until the onion is soft and caramelised.

Add the ginger, garlic, coriander, and spices. Cook for a further 2 minutes.

Mix in the sweetcorn and continue to cook over a low heat until the sweetcorn is cooked.

Remove from the heat. Stir in the lemon juice and the cooked potatoes. Mix well. Adjust the seasoning. Allow to cool.

Once the mixture has cooled, stir in the grated cheese.

To fold the samoosas, start with one sheet lengthways in front of you (narrow end closest).

Brush the farthest end with a little water. Place one heaped teaspoon of the mixture onto the pastry in the corner nearest to you. Begin with the bottom **right** corner (closest to you) and fold diagonally across. Then fold the left bottom end straight up. Then fold the bottom **left** corner diagonally across, and fold the right side up. Repeat until the samoosa is completed, patting down the end-flap brushed with water to secure in place.

Heat 2 to 3 cm of oil in a saucepan or pot. When the oil is very hot, gently place 4 to 6 samoosas into the oil and fry until golden, stirring gently to allow for even browning. Remove with a slotted spoon and drain on kitchen paper.

Serve as a delicious accompaniment to *vegetable curry*.

500 g potatoes, peeled and cubed
vegetable oil for frying
10 ml spice seeds (made up of any
    combination of mustard, cumin,
    coriander, fennel)
3 red onions, sliced
salt
½ tsp turmeric powder
1 tbsp ginger
1 tbsp garlic
½ cup fresh coriander, roughly
    chopped
spices: 5 ml each of cumin,
    coriander, curry powder
½ cup frozen sweetcorn, rinsed
1 tbsp lemon juice
½ cup cheddar cheese, grated
20 sheets samoosa pur
a small bowl of water
pastry brush

Tip

The pastry can be substituted with phyllo pastry, which should be cut with scissors into strips roughly 7 x 20 cm. Because phyllo is thinner than the samoosa pur, it may be easier to double up on sheets and use two at a time.

105

a marriage of flavours

roasted beetroot and butternut, with pan-fried green beans

At lunchtimes, most dishes are served with a selection of fresh seasonal vegetables, lightly steamed and seasoned. Roasted vegetables make for more substantial eating, especially when the weather is cooler. This splendid dish covers most of the basics when it comes to roasting vegetables, and celebrates the delightful marriage of flavours that comes from experimenting in the kitchen – butternut with thyme and mixed spice; and beetroot with rosemary, balsamic vinegar and only the slightest hint of cumin. Because the vegetables are roasted separately, it ensures that the flavours and colours remain distinct and vibrant when serving. A scrumptious dish, enhanced by the added tang of crisp, pan-fried green beans.

Pre-heat the oven to 190°C.

Place the butternut, garlic and thyme in a large mixing bowl. Drizzle with olive oil and season with salt and pepper. Sprinkle with a little paprika and mixed spice. Toss thoroughly until well-coated in olive oil. Place in an oven proof dish or roasting pan.

Combine the beetroot with rosemary and onion. Add the balsamic vinegar, and a pinch of cumin. Season with salt and pepper.

Toss well with olive oil and arrange in a separate roasting dish. Place both dishes in the oven and roast until tender (approximately 50 minutes).

In a wok or large saucepan, heat a small amount of oil. Pan-fry the green beans with sesame seeds, stirring very occasionally so that the beans are flecked.

Add the garlic during the last minutes of cooking to prevent burning. Drizzle with lemon juice and remove from heat. Season with salt and pepper.

Arrange the butternut and beetroot on a serving platter. Top with green beans and serve immediately.

butternut
750 g butternut, peeled and cubed
4-5 garlic cloves, peeled and crushed
4-5 sprigs thyme
olive oil
salt and pepper to taste
paprika
mixed spice

beetroot
750 g beetroot, peeled and cubed
1 tbsp fresh rosemary
4 small red onions, halved (or 2 large onions, quartered)
15 ml balsamic vinegar
cumin
salt and pepper to taste
olive oil

green beans
150 g green beans, topped and tailed
oil for frying
2 tbsp sesame seeds
2 garlic cloves, grated
1 tbsp lemon juice
salt and pepper to taste

ripples 'n reds

sweet and tangy tomato sauce

(serves 4)

The secret to a good tomato-based sauce is never to rush its cooking. Once all the ingredients are added, reduce the heat until only the gentlest of bubbles are rippling at the surface. An hour or two of cooking is perfect; the sauce should be thick and deep red in colour.

Heat the oil in a saucepan. Sauté the onion, until tender.

Add the garlic and bay leaf, and sauté for another 2 minutes.

Add the tomatoes, balsamic vinegar and sugar, and simmer gently, uncovered, until the tomato has cooked.

Adjust the seasoning and serve.

Serve with *millet and corn tortilla*.

olive oil for frying
1 red onion, finely chopped
1 clove garlic, mashed
1 bay leaf
4 large tomatoes, peeled and
  chopped
or 1 tin whole tomatoes,
  chopped
1 tbsp balsamic vinegar
1 tbsp brown sugar
salt and pepper to taste

109

baba ganoush-ish

roasted brinjal and pepper salsa

A liberal variation of the traditional roasted brinjal dip that is a scrumptious topping for baked potatoes. Alternatively, serve with falafel, tortilla crisps or slithers of warm pita bread.

To roast the vegetables, pre-heat the oven to 200°C and grease a baking sheet. Halve the vegetables length-wise (discard pepper seeds and pith). Brush lightly with olive oil and place in a hot oven until the outside skins are charred and the flesh is tender, turning if necessary.

Place the brinjal, tomato, garlic, oil, lemon juice and paprika in a food processor. Blend until well combined, but not completely smooth.

Add the chopped peppers. Pulse-blend until combined (don't over-blend, otherwise you will be left with purée; it should be chunky).

Stir in the chopped coriander. Adjust the seasoning and serve.

Tip
Once the peppers have roasted, place them in a plastic freezer/vegetable bag. Tie, and allow to stand for 10 to 20 minutes. This makes removing the skins a whole lot easier.

(serves 4 to 6)

2 red peppers, roasted and
    peeled, roughly chopped
1 yellow pepper, roasted and
    peeled, roughly chopped
2 brinjals, roasted and peeled
1 tomato, roasted and peeled
1 clove garlic
1 tbsp olive oil
1 tbsp lemon juice
½ tsp paprika
½ tsp smoked paprika
1 tbsp fresh coriander,
    chopped
salt and pepper to taste

grits and greens

pumpkin seed and parsley salsa

(serves 4)

Pumpkin seeds are a delight to cook with because they impart such a unique flavour without demanding a lot of preparation. Toasted seeds have a much more intense flavour and ideally are prepared as needed, but the seeds can also be dry–roasted in a pan and then kept in the refrigerator in a sealed container for later use.

Dry roast the pumpkin seeds in a frying pan. Allow to cool.

Combine all the ingredients in a blender, except for the olive oil. Begin blending and gradually add the olive oil until a paste is formed. Adjust the seasoning.

Serve with *millet and corn tortilla*.

½ cup pumpkin seeds
1 clove garlic
1 green chilli
1 cup parsley, roughly
   chopped
juice of 2 limes
75 ml olive oil (approx.)
salt and pepper to taste
½ tsp ground cumin

hedden's harissa

roasted red pepper harissa

(makes approx. 500 ml)

This North-African sauce gives food a kick it never saw coming. Its dominant fiery taste enhances any dish lucky enough to have it as its companion. I have dedicated the recipe to Sue Hedden who, with her volunteers, heads Woza Moya – the poverty relief and welfare project – providing support and hope to the communities in the valleys around the BRC. My first jar of harissa found its way into every dish Sue ate for the next few weeks – she was so smitten.

Split open the chillies and remove the seeds. Place the skins in a bowl and cover with water; leave to soak until completely hydrated (overnight is best). Wash hands thoroughly after handling the chillies.

Brush the red peppers lightly with olive oil and roast at 200°C until the skins are charred. Remove and place in a plastic bag for 10 minutes. Remove the skins, once cooled.

Drain the chillies and place in a blender with all the other ingredients. Blend until smooth. Adjust the seasoning.

Serve with *falafel* and *couscous*.

50 g dried red chillies
2 red peppers, halved and
    cored
3 cloves garlic
2 teaspoons caraway seeds
1 tbsp ground cumin
2 tsp coriander seeds
1 tsp ground coriander
2 tsp mint, dried or fresh
1 tbsp olive oil
juice of 1 lemon
1 tsp salt

Tips

This is an extremely concentrated sauce. To make a milder paste, use up to half of the chillies and be sure to remove each and every seed. Use to marinate vegetables or tofu, to add fire to any pasta or rice dish, or as a table condiment.
Can be stored in an airtight glass container in the refrigerator for up to 1 month.

113

sangha sag aloo

potato and spinach with cumin

(serves 4 to 6)

Sag aloo literally translates into "spinach with potato". I have added the denotation "sangha", (a gathering of people) to highlight its communal, earthy characteristics. The exclusion of chilli in the recipe makes it a handsomely spiced side-dish, and an interesting contrast when served with a hot, fiery curry. Excellent served with dhal and rice and home-made chutney. The potatoes are pre-cooked so that they mostly retain their shape when mixed with the spinach. Roasting the potatoes beforehand imparts a hearty flavour.

Either deep fry the potatoes or coat lightly with oil and a little salt, and bake at 180°C until golden (do not overcook as the browned potatoes will impart a bitter flavour). Drain on kitchen paper and set aside.

Sauté the onion rings and cumin seeds in the oil until the onion is translucent. Add the tomato, garlic, ginger, and remaining spices (except the garam masala) and stir-fry until the tomato is soft.

Add the spinach and simmer until it is cooked.

Combine the cooked potatoes with the spinach, and mix carefully so as not to break the potato. Season with salt and pepper. Add the lemon juice and garam masala just before serving.

Garnish with lemon rind and chopped coriander.

500 g potatoes, scrubbed,
   peeled and cubed
sunflower oil
1 onion, sliced into rings
1 tsp cumin seeds
1 tomato, chopped
1 tbsp garlic, mashed
1 tbsp ginger, grated
1 tsp paprika
2 tsp cumin powder
1 bunch spinach, washed,
   veined and shredded
salt and pepper to taste
2 tbsp lemon juice
1 tsp garam masala
1 tbsp lemon rind (to garnish)
¼ cup fresh coriander,
   chopped, to garnish

114

smothered in silk

basil tofu mayonnaise

A sensational, dairy-free mayonnaise that works equally well as a dip or a dressing. Delicious served with spring rolls or in a potato salad. Choose silken or soft tofu for an even smoother consistency. Fresh basil is essential, as opposed to dried, but can be substituted with fresh parsley or coriander if not available. For a plain mayonnaise, omit the herbs altogether.

Place all the ingredients in a blender. Blend until smooth.

Keeps well in the refrigerator in a screw-tight jar.

250 ml crumbled tofu
1 clove garlic
100 ml chopped basil
175 ml olive oil
15 ml apple cider vinegar
2 ml mustard
salt
juice of half a lemon
tabasco, optional

Variation
Add 1 tablespoon of green curry paste for a spicy Thai-flavoured mayonnaise.

fabulously feta

greek-style cream 'n chives

(serves 6)

This topping for baked potatoes was created in an attempt to serve something between sour cream with chives, and cottage cheese. If chives are not available, substitute with spring onion greens or even dried dill. Use any left-over sauce as a rich and creamy salad dressing.

Place the cream in a bowl and stir in the lemon juice to sour. Set aside while preparing the rest of the ingredients.

Combine all the ingredients.

Adjust the seasoning and serve.

250 ml fresh cream
1 tbsp fresh lemon juice
1-2 cups plain greek yoghurt
2 tbsp onion, very finely
   chopped
2 tbsp chives, finely
   chopped
½ cup feta cheese, finely
   chopped
salt and pepper to taste

117

green velvet

guacamole (avocado dip)

(serves 4)

Ever popular at the Centre, this light and refreshing dip is so easy to prepare. Choose very ripe avocados for the best flavour and texture.

Mash the avocados until smooth. Add the lime juice, garlic, seasoning and spices.

Stir in the chopped tomato and coriander before serving.

Serve with *baked potatoes*, *millet and corn tortilla*, or *falafel*.

2 avocados, peeled and pitted
juice of 1 lime
1 small clove garlic, mashed
   (optional)
salt and pepper to taste
pinch of cumin and coriander
1 small tomato, chopped
1-2 tsp fresh coriander,
   chopped

nalanda rocks

buckwheat and coriander blinis

(serves 6)

Of the many walks around the Centre, some of the most spectacular views of the valley are from Nalanda, a rocky outcrop that protrudes precariously from the mountainside in layered, flat platforms. The rocks are named after the ruins of an ancient Buddhist monastery, library and study centre that were destroyed in India in the 10th CE. These delectable savouries with their rich earthen colouring and flat, amorphous shapes are reminiscent of these rocks. They make an interesting gluten-free accompaniment to soup, or can be served with sour cream and any number of toppings to make delightful finger-food.

1 cup buckwheat flour
2 tsp baking powder
pinch ground coriander
½ tsp salt
black pepper
2 eggs, lightly beaten
4 tbsp milk (approx.)
2 tbsp fresh coriander, chopped
1 small tomato, chopped
vegetable oil for frying

Combine the flour, baking powder, ground coriander, salt and pepper in a mixing bowl.

Add the eggs and gradually add the milk, 1 tablespoon at a time, until a thick batter is formed.

Add the fresh coriander and tomato, and mix well.

Heat a small amount of oil in a frying pan over a moderately high heat.

Drop tablespoons of batter into the pan. Fry for approximately 1 minute on each side until golden.

Serve with *butter jade soup* or with sour cream and various vegetable toppings such as spring onions, sprouts and grated carrot.

zesty zen zinger

fruity tamarind chutney

(makes approx. 500 ml)

Do not be put off by the long list of ingredients in this chutney. Its preparation is really very simple and it will keep almost indefinitely in a sealed container in the refrigerator. Remember that the mixture will continue to set as it cools, so what may look like slightly runny chutney, when cooked, will settle into a thick and jam-like consistency on standing. If the chutney is too thick after cooling, water it down with a little boiling water. Excellent with curries, but also makes a superb sandwich pickle or veggie burger relish.

Place the onions, garlic, tomato, half the raisins, chilli and ginger in a blender or food processor. Blend until a paste is formed.

Heat the oil in a large saucepan and sauté the onion mixture for 2 to 3 minutes.

Add all the remaining ingredients and simmer for approximately 50 minutes, until the chutney is thick and glossy and has a jam-like consistency.

Serve hot or cold.

Tips

If seedless tamarind is unavailable, prepare conventional tamarind in the following way.
Place the tamarind in a heat-proof bowl and cover with 1 cup of boiling water. Stir vigorously with a fork until a thick brown liquid is formed. Strain this liquid into the saucepan.

Return the tamarind to the bowl and repeat with the remaining water until every last drop of goodness has been squished out of the pulp.
(Remember to count how many cups of water have been added as this will make up the liquid quantity for the chutney.)

2 large onions, peeled and
    roughly chopped
2 cloves garlic, peeled
1 tomato
1 cup raisins
1 green chilli
2 tbsp ginger, roughly chopped
1 tbsp cooking oil
1 cup brown sugar
½ cup apple cider vinegar
100 g seedless tamarind paste
1 large granny smith apple,
    peeled and grated
1 cup grated carrot
¼ cup fresh coriander leaves,
    chopped
1 tbsp ground paprika
1 tbsp ground coriander
1 tbsp ground cinnamon
1-2 star aniseed
1 tbsp coarse sea salt
pepper to taste
4 cups water (approx.)

119

Stone Bowls at Ixopo

stone bowls brim
with water everywhere.
at doorways, pergolas,
near the gong, bridge,
sleep and sitting space.

in one basin, a leaf
floats, tinted pink
as winter sunset.
and below that –
or is it above –
in reflection
the leaves
on the branch
it floated from
still bloom.

beyond these leaves,
deeper and higher,
scudding clouds shift
through today's sky.
they part a moment
to offer a shred of blue.
and we like this lone leaf
lie silent in a ripple of change.
(DH)

into the cauldron

caramelised baby onions

(serves 4 to 6)

Somewhere between a side dish and chutney, this has become an absolute staple with our *good shepherd's pie*. Producing this dish makes you feel like an alchemist preparing a magic potion. The ingredients are added to the pot one at a time, and left to simmer and stew. Then you stand back, smell the heady vapours and watch the contents transform themselves into a flavourful, enchanted brew.

Place all the ingredients, except the onions, in a flat saucepan and stir over a low heat until combined.

Add the onions and a little extra water if they are not quite covered. Bring to the boil, and then simmer uncovered for up to 1 hour until the sauce is thick and the onions are cooked through.

¼ cup apple cider vinegar

30 ml olive oil

3 tbsp brown sugar

30 g tomato paste

1 bay leaf

¼ cup parsley, chopped

½ cup raisins

1 green chilli (optional)

½ tsp mixed spice

1 star aniseed

1½ cups water

salt and pepper to taste

500 g baby onions, peeled

Floating in a Bowl

three wedges rest
on an oak cutting board
as if arranged in a still life.

an apple slice lies
rose-skinned, quartered
with pips and core.

a lemon skin ring
rims the wheel
of cell and rind.

knobbed gingerroot
flexes rhizome muscles
like a samurai.

then a hand drops
each gift into the pitcher.
they swirl in the stream.

as they rise, fall, float,
they magnify and move
through the glass heart.

the apple blossoms,
the lemon offers its tang,
the ginger breathes spice.

they refract light to infuse
and enliven in zen scent
bubbles of delight.
(DH)

st anthony's fire

brinjal atchaar

(serves 6)

While I cooked at the Centre, Anthony Shapiro, the internationally renowned potter, was the artist in residence. He remains a close friend of mine – and the Centre. His exquisitely crafted bowls and platters display our vegetables, curries, salads and desserts. Whenever I had tried out something new, it became something of a ritual to run a sample down to his pottery studio for feedback. His hands dripping with clay, he would savour it contemplatively and pronounce on it. His verdict was always spot-on. This atchaar got a big thumbs-up from Anthony, and has been a permanent fixture on the menu ever since. It is the perfect pickle for pyromaniacs.

Prepare the brinjals.

Place the garlic, ginger and spices in a blender and add enough oil to form a thick paste.

Heat the oil in a saucepan. Add the brinjals (rinse first, if salted) and stir gently until golden.

Add the paste, green chilli and salt; stir for another 2 minutes.

Reduce the heat and simmer gently until cooked.

Add the lemon juice and lemon zest.

Serve warm, or bottle and store refrigerated for up to 1 month.

Essential eating with a good curry, and heavenly with cheese, salad and our *BRC brown bread*.

1 kg baby brinjals, quartered
  (and salted, if desired)
6 cloves garlic
2 tbsp ginger, grated
1 tbsp atchaar spice
1 tbsp garam masala
1 tbsp turmeric
1 cup sunflower oil, plus extra
  for paste
1 fresh green chilli (seeded, if
  desired)
1 tsp salt
2 tbsp lemon juice
1 tsp lemon zest

123

Tips

Atchaar spice is a fiery blend of spices, including red chilli and coriander seeds, and is available at most Indian supermarkets. If you cannot find atchaar spice, use a hot curry powder instead. When making the atchaar, squeeze the lemon into the mixture and then just pop the half lemon directly into the pot instead of adding the zest.

the sweet stuff of legends

our famous apple and mango chutney

(makes 500 ml)

Curry is something of a Sunday lunch staple at the Centre. It is a veritable feast served with an adventurous mix of accompaniments and sambals. No curry is ever complete, however, without a bowl of this appetising chutney straight from the stove to complete this culinary spectacle. Since the recipe calls for dried mangoes, it is an excellent winter relish to make when mangoes are no longer in season, but apples are in abundance. Store any leftovers (if there are any) in the refrigerator, and thin with a little boiling water if needed to re-serve.

Brown the cumin seeds and star aniseed in oil over a medium heat until the cumin is golden. Add the apples, ginger and turmeric. Sauté for 2 minutes.

Add the remaining ingredients. Bring to the boil and then simmer for 40 to 50 minutes until thickened and the sugar has caramelised.

The chutney keeps in the refrigerator for up to 3 months.

1 tbsp sunflower oil
1 tsp cumin seeds
2 star aniseed
250 g green apples, peeled, cored and sliced
1 tbsp ginger, grated
1 tsp turmeric
8 sticks dried mango, cut into small pieces
1 cup water (approx.)
1 tbsp apple cider vinegar
½ tsp cinnamon
½ tsp ground coriander
salt and pepper to taste
2 cups brown sugar

sunshine on the cob

grilled sweetcorn mealies with sweet chilli, coriander and lime

A zesty accompaniment to festive summer meals that can either be oven-grilled or cooked on the braai. Par-boiling the mealies enables you to grill them quickly. This prevents them from drying out. Cut the mealies into smaller pieces that are easier to handle, but take care when cutting the cobs as they are quite tough. Use a very sharp knife.

Pre-heat the oven to 220°C or set to grill.

Place the mealies in a pot with boiling water and par-boil for 15 minutes.

Melt the butter in a saucepan with the oil. Add the spices and sweet chilli sauce, and bring to the boil. Add the garlic and cook while stirring for 5 minutes until thick. Add the lime juice and chopped coriander. Adjust the seasoning and set aside.

Arrange the mealies in a roasting pan. Spoon over half of the chilli mixture and place on highest rack in oven. When the mealies start to brown, remove from the oven. Turn the cobs over using a fork or tongs. Spoon over the remaining mixture and return to the oven until grilled on both sides.

Garnish with a little extra chopped coriander and serve.

1 kg sweetcorn mealies (about 6), cleaned and cut into thirds
50 g butter
¼ cup olive oil
½ tsp cumin seeds
½ tsp coriander seeds, crushed
¼ cup sweet chilli sauce
1 tbsp garlic, mashed
1 tbsp lime juice
½ cup fresh coriander, chopped
salt and pepper to taste

125

Tip
To barbecue the mealies, par-boil as normal. Toss the cobs in half of the sauce and brush with the remaining sauce while grilling on the braai.

sweets

clouds across the moon

apple crumble

One of the more popular desserts served at the Centre. The secret is to work gently with the flour mixture to create perfect crumbs which are then sprinkled delicately over the apple slices. The recipe can be made with fresh or tinned apples, but using fresh apples allows you to be creative with the flavouring added to the cooking water. Cinnamon is standard, but try cardamom pods, star aniseed or nutmeg to create a crumble that is extra special and has your signature on it.

500 g self-raising flour
½ tsp each of cinnamon, mixed
   spice and cardamom
pinch nutmeg
½ tsp salt
250 g butter, soft
2 cups brown sugar
500 g apples, cooked
   (or 1 x 725 g tin)
½ cup raisins
½ cup chopped nuts

Pre-heat the oven to 180°C and grease an oven-proof dish.

Work the flour, spices, salt and butter together between your thumbs and fingertips to form crumbs.

Add the sugar and blend with your fingers to retain the consistency of breadcrumbs.

Combine half the mixture with the apples and raisins, and place in a dish.

Sprinkle over the remaining crumbs and then repeat with the chopped nuts.

Bake for 45 minutes until golden.

Serve with cream or a generous dollop of homemade custard.

banoffee pie

banana and caramel pie

(serves 12)

This is the BRC version of this famous pie. You can make caramelised condensed milk by removing the label from a tin of condensed milk and boiling it in plenty of water for 2 hours. It is essential that the pot never runs out of water, so keep a kettle handy to top up as you go. Allow the tin to cool completely before opening. Commercially bought caramel is far more convenient, but does lack some of the velvety texture of the home-made caramel.

200 g digestive biscuits
60 ml butter, melted (approx.)
360 g tin caramel treat
6 medium bananas, sliced
500 ml fresh cream, whipped
cinnamon or drinking
  chocolate, to garnish

129

Pulse the biscuits in a blender until they resemble breadcrumbs.

Combine well with the melted butter and press down gently into a serving dish. Place in the refrigerator for at least 20 minutes to set.

Using a spatula, gently spread the caramel over the biscuit base in an even layer.

Place the sliced banana over the caramel to form a banana layer.

Top with whipped cream, and smooth with a spatula.

Sprinkle lightly with cinnamon or drinking chocolate and return to the refrigerator for at least 30 minutes before serving.

Candle Power

tonight the power cut out
at this retreat. no moon. all silent.
I am sole sleeper in the centre's hut,
no other body within a circle of 300
steps.

I take a white-robed tea cup
find three candles, visit the lemon tree,
pluck a moon, slice it into crescents,
embed, wedge them around the sticks.

a trilogy of light leaps from the cup
a thin film separates their flames,
these three heads-together sisters
turn the bedside table into an altar.

flame shade, between candle white
and yellow skin, flickers
then climbs from its knees, steady.
illuminates the halo, a pip ablaze.

lemon juice rises up the ribs
of the mystic sisters, melting,
scenting the wax, burning the bitter,
fruiting the flame, becoming one.
(DH)

autumnal notes

pumpkin lagaan with rosewater cream

(serves 6 to 8)

This baked dessert is best made with butternut or sweet potato when pumpkin is not available, and is deliciously gluten-free. The addition of rose-flavoured pouring cream makes it a sensuous Eastern delight. For the right consistency, mix all the ingredients together except the milk. Gradually add the milk while stirring until the mixture has the consistency of a thick dropping batter. Do not panic if you have added too much milk; simply adjust the consistency by adding a little extra rice flour.

Combine all the ingredients in a large mixing bowl.

Pour into a greased ovenproof dish.

Sprinkle liberally with poppy seeds and flaked almonds.

Bake at 180°C for 45 to 50 minutes, until golden brown.

For the rosewater cream, whisk all the ingredients together until the sugar (or honey) has dissolved.

Adjust the flavouring.

4 cups pumpkin or sweet
  potato (boiled and mashed)
90 ml melted butter
3 cups desiccated coconut
3 cups milk (approx.)
2 cups sugar
4 large eggs
2 tbsp baking powder
1 tsp ground cardamom
½ cup rice flour
poppy seeds and flaked
  almonds to garnish

rosewater cream
250 ml fresh cream
1 tbsp rosewater
1 tbsp brown sugar (or honey)
½ tsp ground cardamom

131

square waltz

chocolate pecan squares

(makes 24)

A symphony of favourite baked flavours, topped with the most decadent of icings. What I love about this recipe is that it always keeps perfect timing – it is literally to the minute that it bakes to perfection in the oven. The recipe makes enough for 24 squares. Lightly toast the chopped pecans in a dry non-stick pan until lightly browned and aromatic.

Pre-heat the oven to 180°C and grease a 23 cm long baking tray.

Melt the butter in a saucepan over a low heat.

Once the butter has melted, remove from the heat and add the sifted flours, sugar, coconut and cocoa powder. Stir until well combined.

Add the egg and mix well.

Place the mixture in the baking tray and press down gently until evenly distributed. Bake for approximately 20 minutes until firm to the touch and the mixture is coming away slightly from the sides of the tray.

Combine all the icing ingredients, except the nuts, to form a thick, but spreadable paste. Add a little extra milk (1 teaspoon at a time) if the mixture is too thick, until the desired consistency has been reached.

Spread the icing over the baked mixture while still hot.

Sprinkle with chopped pecans and press gently into the icing to fix in place.

Allow to cool for 15 minutes before cutting into squares, using a sharp knife.

Allow to cool completely in the tray before serving.

250 g butter
1 cup cake flour
2/3 cup self-raising flour
1 cup brown sugar
2 cups coconut
3 tbsp cocoa powder
2 eggs, lightly beaten

icing
2 cups icing sugar, sifted
3 tbsp cocoa powder
2 tsp soft butter
4 tbsp milk
2 cups chopped pecans

133

the milky way

crustless milk tart

(makes 15 squares)

The secret behind this recipe is to get as much air into the egg whites as possible. The egg white mixture loses air as soon as you stop beating, so make sure that you get the egg whites into the bowl with the other ingredients and into the oven as soon as possible. The method is also a great metaphor for life – to keep it light. Don't worry if the mixture is watery when you put it in the oven. A beautiful alchemy occurs when, with the heat, the mixture is transformed into a mouth-watering treat.

4 eggs, separated
1 cup sugar
60 g melted butter
1 cup cake flour
1 tsp baking powder
pinch of salt
1 litre milk
1 tsp vanilla

cinnamon sugar
50 ml sugar
level tsp cinnamon

Grease 1 large oven-proof dish.

Beat the egg yolks, sugar, and butter until creamy.

Sift the cake flour, baking powder and salt and add to the yolk mixture.

Add the milk and vanilla, and mix well.

Beat the egg whites until firm.

Using a metal spoon, fold them into the milk mixture – the mixture is very thin.

Pour into the dish, and sprinkle with cinnamon sugar.

Bake at 180°C for 40 to 50 minutes.

Slice into squares and serve warm or cold.

summer layers

greek mango dessert

(serves 4 to 6)

Serve this delectable dessert in a glass bowl for the full impact of the layers of vibrant orange and stark white, shot through with streaks of caramel syrup. Pecan nuts, sprinkled on top, add just the right finishing touch and a wonderful crunchiness.

250 ml fresh cream
250 ml greek yoghurt
30 ml brown sugar
5 ml cinnamon
3 mangoes, peeled and
   cubed
nuts for garnishing
   (optional)

Beat the cream until stiff. Add the yoghurt, sugar and cinnamon and fold in carefully.

In the serving bowl, place alternate layers of mango and the cream and yoghurt mixture, ending with a layer of cream and yoghurt.

Sprinkle with cinnamon and sugar and garnish with chopped nuts.

Refrigerate for at least 4 hours before serving.

Variations
Instead of the sugar, add a quarter of a teaspoon of vanilla essence to the yoghurt and cream mixture. Top with treacle sugar, cover with cling-film and allow to caramelise in the refrigerator. Before serving, decorate with toasted flaked almonds.

ixopocabana

tropical fruit salad

A refreshingly simple fruit salad with an exotic twist. The quantities are really just a guide. The simple way to make the recipe is to pour the juice into a large bowl with the "seasoning" and then keep adding fruit until filled. Make sure that the fruit is still covered with juice. Enjoy on its own or with a splash of coconut cream.

Combine all the ingredients in a large bowl.
Adjust the flavouring and refrigerate until needed.

1 litre tropical fruit juice (pure, unsweetened)
80 ml granadilla pulp (or 1 tin)
2 tbsp ginger, grated
1-2 tbsp rosewater
3 tbsp fresh mint, finely chopped
6 cups mixed fruit (pineapple, melon, kiwi, banana, mango, papaya etc.)

rumi rounds

rose and cardamom slicing biscuits

137

This recipe is inspired by the Persian "love poet" Rumi. Roses are scarce at the Centre and when they are available, they beg to be revered in a memorable way. The addition of fresh rose petals transforms a simple biscuit into a glorious tea-time treat. Is there any greater sensual combination than that of freshly-ground cardamom and the blissful scent of roses? The mixture can be made well in advance and stored in the refrigerator or freezer, and sliced and baked as needed.

Cream the butter, icing sugar, salt and rose essence, until light and fluffy.
Add the flour and cardamom and mix well.
Add the rose petals and knead lightly until combined.
Roll into a "sausage" shape, roughly 4 cm thick. Cover with cling-film, place on a tray and refrigerate overnight.
Grease a baking sheet and pre-heat the oven to 180°C.
Slice the biscuits into 1 cm slices, using a very sharp knife. Place on a baking sheet and bake for 15 minutes until lightly golden. Sprinkle with castor sugar.

200 g butter, soft
100 g icing sugar, sifted
pinch of salt
rose essence
300 g self-raising flour, sifted
1 tsp ground cardamom
rose petals (approx. 12)
castor sugar

Tips
Keep refrigerated for up to one week, or freeze for up to one month.
Be sure to use fresh, unsprayed rose petals only. Commercially grown roses are usually heavily treated with a number of chemicals.

triple gem cookies

cranberry and macadamia biscuits

(makes 24)

Among all the trees at the Centre, the macadamia tree is special to all who live there. I originally created this recipe using almonds, but once I had made the biscuits with macadamia nuts from our tree I knew there was no turning back. Before baking, three nuts are pressed into each cookie as a small reminder of the three jewels offered as refuge in Buddhist practice – namely the Buddha, the Dharma and the Sangha.

100 g macadamia nuts, ground
250 g self-raising flour
1 tsp baking powder
100 g oats
50 g dried cranberries
250 g butter, soft
100 g castor sugar
100 g brown sugar
macadamia pieces, for
   decoration

Pre-heat the oven to 180°C and grease 2 to 3 baking sheets.

Grind the nuts in a food processor and then toast lightly in a dry pan, until golden.

Sift the flour and baking powder into a bowl, and stir in the oats, ground nuts and cranberries.

In a separate bowl, beat together the butter and sugars until light and fluffy.

Combine with the flour mixture and knead gently until well combined.

Roll into balls approximately 3 cm in diameter.

Place on the baking tray. Press down lightly, and then press in three macadamia pieces for decoration. Be sure to leave enough space between the biscuits as they spread out during baking (about 9 on a sheet).

Bake for 12 to 15 minutes or until lightly golden.

Remove from the heat and allow to cool on the trays for 5 minutes, before lifting gently with a spatula and placing on cooling racks.

The biscuits will keep for up to 1 week in an airtight container.

Gong at a Retreat Centre

These hills are grass-covered and rolling...
lovely beyond any singing... (Alan Paton)

along a stone path,
on a nail and rough string,
the gong dangles in the wind.
It sways between
the place of silence,
sitting in the hall
and the quiet pages
of the rondavel library.

the wooden pestle
stirs this mortar,
pebbles its circle sound
across this lotus lake.
it gathers at this Zen bridge,
statues, garden, shrine,
garden of greens,
and echoes in soup ladle,
bread oven, water jug
and the valley and hills
lovely beyond singing.

standing here, I become
suspended emptiness
in a cylinder of sound –
tube brother to Tibetan bells,
tingshaw discs on leather thong,
humming rim of bowl.

the first metal sounding
echoes my birth,
the second, presence,
and the third striking,
will be for disappearing
as the core of silence
ghosts awhile within,
then gongs me
into another being.
(DH)

thoroughly speckled

chocolate almond salami

(serves 6)

Another popular tea-time treat at the Centre. These convenient rolls can be made the day before and then refrigerated overnight (or frozen until needed). Do not be alarmed by the consistency of the mixture. Even when we made these for the first time, it felt like the mixture was too dry. The salami needs to have this consistency in order to be shaped into rolls. Use a very sharp knife to cut into slices. Cut pressing down, instead of moving the knife back and forth, for the best speckled effect.

Mix all the ingredients together, except the biscuits and ground almonds.

Add the crushed biscuits and mix until well combined.

Use 2 sheets of wax paper and place half of the mixture on the sheets.

Roll in the paper until a "sausage" shape is formed.

On a clean sheet of wax paper, sprinkle ground almonds and a little brown sugar.

Coat the salami in the sugar and almonds.

Repeat with the remaining mixture to make two rolls.

Wrap in wax paper and place in the freezer until needed.

Defrost for approximately 1 hour before slicing with a very sharp, small knife into 1 cm slices.

200 g drinking chocolate
50 g cocoa powder
200 g castor sugar
2 tbsp melted butter
2 eggs
almond essence (just a few drops)
200 g tea biscuits (marie), crushed
50 g ground almonds, toasted
brown sugar, for sprinkling

141

the cake the buddha ate

carrot cake, with a story

Maybe someone played a trick on me. Maybe I am gullible, but I am convinced that the bronze Buddha in my home shrine ate a piece of this cake! The full story is told in the introduction to this recipe book. A firm favourite, this scrumptious cake is served at most morning tea-times during weekend retreats at the Centre. Be adventurous with spices such as cardamom, cloves, allspice or nutmeg.

Pre-heat the oven to 180°C and grease two 20 cm cake pans.

Beat the sugar, oil, eggs, vanilla essence and salt together in a large mixing bowl.

Sift the flour, bicarbonate of soda and cinnamon into this mixture and blend thoroughly.

Add the rest of the ingredients and mix. Pour the batter into the cake pans and bake for 45 to 60 minutes. When a skewer inserted into the cake comes out clean, it is ready.

For the icing, combine the icing sugar, cream cheese, soft butter, lemon juice, and lemon and orange zest. Add teaspoons of water, if necessary, until the icing is thick and pliable.

Decorate with crushed walnuts or pecan nuts.

750 ml brown sugar
375 ml sunflower oil
4 eggs (extra large)
12.5 ml vanilla essence
5 ml salt
750 ml cake flour
12.5 ml bicarbonate of soda
12.5 ml ground cinnamon
375 ml chopped walnuts or
   pecan nuts
375 ml desiccated coconut
375 ml carrots, cooked and
   puréed
180 ml crushed pineapple,
   drained

icing
2 cups icing sugar
100 ml cream cheese
30 ml soft butter
5 ml lemon juice
5 ml lemon zest
5 ml orange zest

143

golden kisses

chocolate, cornflake and almond kisses

Cornflakes are a wonderful base for making these delicious gluten-free
nibbly bits. This is a simple dessert that is quick and easy to whip up
without having to trawl the pantry for ingredients. The tricky part is
giving these clusters enough time to set in the fridge without nibbling
on them beforehand. Using dairy-free dark chocolate, creates a delicious
vegan treat.

Toast the almonds in a dry pan until golden.

Gently melt the butter, syrup and chocolate in a small, heavy pan.

Stir in the cornflakes and the almonds.

Place spoonfuls of the mixture into individual paper cups and arrange
on a baking sheet.

Leave to set in the refrigerator for at least 1 hour.

(makes 24)

50 g nibbed almonds, toasted
50 g butter
4 tbsp golden syrup
1 bar plain chocolate (100 g)
75 g cornflakes
small paper cake cups

summer tang

lemon and ginger cheesecake

(serves 6 to 8)

A light and breezy fridge-cake with a refreshing zing of lemon and ginger. Be mindful of not pressing the biscuit base down too firmly, otherwise it will set solid and your moment of glory will be dampened when your guests have to chisel out a slice from the serving dish. It is the lemon juice that works to set this dessert, so time in the refrigerator is needed. For a cheesecake that needs to be whipped up in a matter of hours, use the agar flakes which are available from all wholefood stores, and which act as a vegetable-based gelatine to help the process along.

200 g digestive biscuits
4 tbsp butter (approx.) melted
125 ml lemon juice
250 ml condensed milk
250 ml smooth cream cheese
2 tbsp ginger, grated
1 tbsp agar flakes (optional)
250 ml fresh cream

Crush the biscuits in a food processor until they resemble coarse breadcrumbs.

Place in a flat serving dish. Pour over the melted butter.

Combine until the crumbs just stick together. Press down gently to line the dish.

In a large mixing bowl, combine all other ingredients, except the cream, and whisk until smooth.

Whip the cream to a firm peak stage.

Fold gently into the mixture.

Pour into the dish and refrigerate for at least 8 hours.

delectable dainty dollops

buckwheat flapjacks with mediterranean compote

A delightful dessert that also makes a decadent breakfast. Serve the flapjacks with yoghurt, figs and mint in separate bowls so that each person can create his own "D-I-Y" delight.

flapjacks

Combine the flour, baking powder, sugar, cinnamon and salt in a mixing bowl.

Add the eggs and vanilla extract. Gradually add the milk, 1 tablespoon at a time, until a thick batter is formed.

Heat a small amount of oil in a frying pan over a moderately high heat.

Drop tablespoons of batter into the pan.

Fry for approximately 1 minute on each side, until golden.

compote

Place the water, cinnamon, honey and sugar in a saucepan. Dissolve the sugar completely before bringing to a boil. Reduce, without stirring, to half the quantity.

Add the figs and simmer for 5 minutes.

Remove from the heat and add the nuts.

Serve the compote on the flapjacks with a dollop of thick yoghurt.

Garnish with fresh mint.

flapjacks

1 cup buckwheat flour
2 tsp baking powder
3 tbsp brown sugar
1 tsp ground cinnamon
pinch of salt
2 eggs, lightly beaten
vanilla extract (a few drops)
5 tbsp milk (approx.)
oil for frying

147

compote

1 cup water
1 cinnamon stick
1 tbsp honey
½ cup brown sugar (muscovado)
100 g dried figs, soaked and
    quartered
100 g nuts, chopped
greek yoghurt
chopped mint (optional)

spaza slice

quick and easy bread and butter pudding

(serves 6)

This is an excellent pudding to make for those who have either limited equipment or limited space, because all the ingredients are mixed directly into the baking dish and then folded together with a fork. This is David's recipe which he could whip up with impressive speed. On days when a trip to town was not on the cards, David would gladly hop on his bike down to the local valley "spaza" (kiosk) to buy a loaf of fine, ready-sliced white bread which, for some incomprehensible reason, always tasted better than anything bought at a supermarket. This is comfort food at its best.

9 slices white bread
100 g butter, soft (approx.)
3 cups milk
¾ cup brown sugar
6 eggs
¼ cup desiccated coconut
½ cup raisins
½ cup flaked almonds
1 tsp vanilla essence
½ tsp nutmeg
pinch of salt
cinnamon for sprinkling

149

Butter the bread with soft butter on one side.

Pour the milk and sugar into an oven-proof dish, and stir until the sugar is dissolved.

Add the eggs, coconut, raisins, almonds, vanilla essence, nutmeg and salt. Use a fork to lightly whisk the eggs and the other ingredients together.

Arrange the slices of bread, buttered side up, into the dish and press down with a fork to absorb the liquid.

Use the fork to gently fold all of the ingredients, breaking up the bread slightly and combining with the raisins and almonds.

Allow to stand for 30 minutes (or refrigerate overnight).

Pre-heat the oven to 180°C. Sprinkle with cinnamon and bake for 45 minutes until golden.

Serve immediately.

rosie's rise 'n shine

banana nut crunch muffins

These marvellous muffins make for extraordinary breakfasting and are best served ever so slightly cooled while the topping still has its maximum crunchiness. The secret is to mix the wet and dry muffin ingredients together until they are just combined and still a little lumpy, before spooning them into the pan.

muffins

Preheat the oven to 180°C and grease a muffin pan.

Sift the flours and return the bran to the bowl. Combine with the sugar, baking powder and spices.

In a separate bowl, combine the egg, buttermilk, mashed bananas, and oil.

Add the wet ingredients to the dry, and mix until just combined (the mixture should look lumpy; if it is over-mixed, the muffins will not rise).

Spoon into muffin trays and spoon over teaspoonfuls of the crunchy topping mixture on the top.

topping

For the topping, combine the butter with the nuts, and then stir in the sugar.

Garnish with a whole pecan nut and bake for 20 minutes until golden brown.

1 cup nutty wheat flour
1 cup cake flour
1/3 cup brown sugar
4 tsp baking powder
¼ tsp mixed spice
¼ tsp cinnamon
1 egg, lightly beaten
1 cup buttermilk
3-4 bananas, mashed (the riper the better)
¼ cup sunflower oil
whole pecan nuts

topping
50 g butter, melted
¾ cup mixed nuts, chopped (almonds, pecans and brazils work well)
¼ cup brown sugar

151

winter warmth

baked fruit pudding

This decadent winter pudding is an excellent stand-by when fresh fruit is not available. While the pudding is baking, make the sauce so that it can be added to the hot pudding straight from the oven. We prefer pecan or macadamia nuts for this pudding, but use whatever nuts are available.

Pre-heat the oven to 190°C and grease a large oven-proof dish.

Sift the flour, baking powder, bicarbonate of soda and salt into a large bowl. Add the remaining ingredients one at a time until a thick batter is formed. Add a little of the reserved fruit liquid, if the mixture is dry.

Pour into the dish and bake for 50 to 55 minutes until cooked through.

Remove from the oven and poke with a fork to make a series of holes throughout the pudding.

Pour over the sauce and allow to cool slightly before serving.

For the sauce, combine all the ingredients, except the zest, in a saucepan. Bring to the boil, stirring continuously to dissolve the sugar. Boil for 5 minutes until thick and creamy.

Remove from the heat and add the zest before pouring over the pudding.

Serve with cream.

pudding
3 cups flour
1 tbsp baking powder
1 tbsp bicarbonate of soda
1 tsp salt
2 cups brown sugar
3 eggs, lightly beaten
500 g tin fruit cocktail, drained
   (reserve the liquid)
½ cup raisins
½ cup nuts, chopped
1 tsp mixed spice

sauce
1½ cups sugar
4 tbsp butter (60 ml)
1 cup desiccated coconut
1 cup milk
2 tbsp ginger, grated
1 tbsp citrus zest (orange and
   lemon)

153

cry, the beloved crunchies

the famous brc crunchies

These mouth-watering crunchies have become a staple offering at weekend tea-times. Be sure to make them in large quantities because you will want to share them with friends, family, and even the neighbours (besides, the recipe is so much easier to measure out when making two trays). A good thing about these crunchies is that they encourage experimentation and yet remain virtually flop-proof. Use a combination of various nuts and seeds to make up the two cups.

Heat the oven to 160°C and grease 2 baking sheets.

Melt the butter in a saucepan. Add the peanut butter and syrup. Dissolve.

Combine all the other ingredients, except the bicarbonate of soda, in a large bowl.

Once the butter starts to bubble gently, remove from the heat. Stir in the bicarbonate of soda and add to the dry mixture. Combine well. (Hands work best, and make for extremely satisfying work.)

Press into the baking trays, and bake for 20 minutes until golden brown.

Cut into squares with a very sharp knife, while still warm.

500 g butter
2 tbsp peanut butter
2 tbsp syrup
3 cups cake flour
2 cups oats
2 cups muesli
2 cups brown sugar
2 cups desiccated coconut
2 cups chopped nuts
    (pecans, cashews,
    almonds, macadamia etc)
or 2 cups mixed seeds
    (pumpkin, sunflower,
    sesame, poppy seeds)
2 tsp mixed spice
2 tsp bicarbonate of soda

Variation

Replace the syrup with honey,
the peanut butter with tahini,
and use 2 cups of sesame seeds.

155

a moment's pause

lemon, ginger and coconut slices

(makes 12)

The BRC is always buzzing with activity. Sometimes the best chance to catch up with the goings-on of the day is over a quick cup of tea. With the addition of something heavenly from the kitchen, it creates the perfect opportunity to pause and take a moment to enjoy these zesty slices.

Pre-heat the oven to 180°C and grease a roasting pan or baking tray.

Melt the butter and honey in a saucepan.

Combine the dry ingredients and ginger in a mixing bowl.

Remove the butter from the heat and stir into the dry ingredients. Once combined, add the egg and mix well.

Press into the baking dish and bake for 25 to 30 minutes until golden.

Combine the icing ingredients one at a time, adding teaspoons of water until smooth and thick.

Once the cake has cooled from the oven, spread the icing over the top.

Slice into squares.

Garnish with extra lemon zest.

60 g butter
1 tbsp honey
1½ cups self-raising flour
½ cup brown sugar
½ cup desiccated coconut
2 tbsp ginger, grated
1 egg

icing
1 cup icing sugar, sifted
2 tbsp butter, melted
1 tbsp lemon juice
1 tbsp ginger, grated
1 tsp lemon zest
1 tsp hot water (approx.)

157

A stupa for Nkulunkulu

Better known as a pagoda in the Chinese and Japanese Buddhist cultures, the stupa symbolises a number of Buddhist philosophical principles. They often contain relics and sacred scriptures. You will find them in their thousands, scattered around the countryside in the Far East.

I had a window of only three weeks to build this stupa – just me and two helpers. As I was building the base and the dome, I pondered how to construct the complicated spire. Then it struck me. I went to a garden shop and bought a selection of concrete planters of various sizes. I threaded them onto a steel pipe, some up-side-down, and surmounted them with a finial made of several brass Hindu ceremonial vessels welded together. These act as a lightning conductor. Maybe all this was a bit prosaic. But the stupa was completed on time.

I had left an opening in the dome so that I could extract the scaffolding that propped up the upper part of the stupa. When I proceeded to brick it up, my Induna (foreman) stopped me: "How can anyone get in without a door?" But he seemed satisfied with my answer. "The stupa," I said, "was a home for Nkulunkulu (God), who could go anywhere and pass through everything." There would be nothing else of any value inside it.

Still, someone from the valley must have suspected otherwise and tried to tunnel into it soon after the stupa's inauguration. They were stopped by the solid rock on which it is built...

The Buddha's nose
on a platter

I had never done any sculpting before I undertook to build the statue – upon a challenge by a visiting monk, Ajahn Anando. So I asked Peter Schütz, an internationally renowned sculptor and good friend of mine, to help me model the face. But he only offered to do the nose for me. Why only the nose, I never found out. You could never be sure you could take Peter seriously.

He was a busy man, lecturing at university and forever preparing pieces for exhibitions of his work. So I was left on my own. I had to complete the five meter high statue myself, including the face. And the nose.

Years later, the Buddha statue completed, Peter had a run of exhibitions in which he explored the many-layered interface between baroque saints and the symbolism of the "dumbwaiter". One day he turned up at my house, with his customary bottle of red wine in one hand and a parcel, wrapped in brown paper, in the other. He gave it to me with a shy smile.

It was a "dumbwaiter", offering the Buddha's nose on a platter...

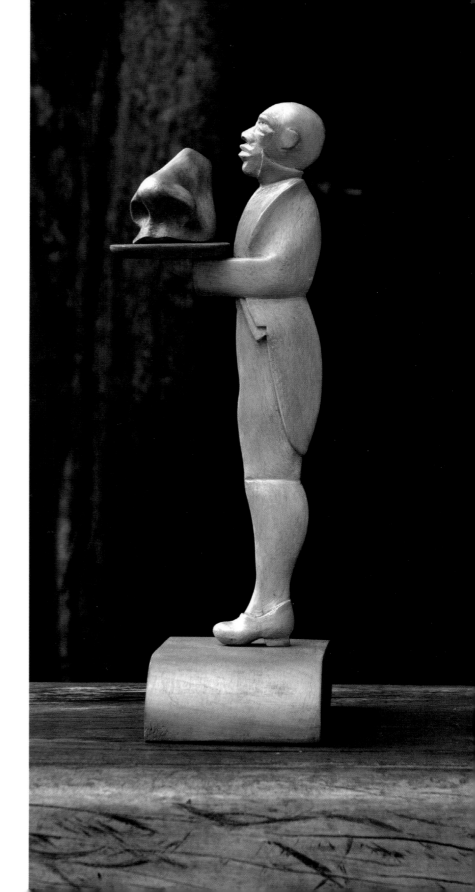

breads

at the golden shrine

banana bread

(makes 1 loaf)

The Buddhist Retreat Centre is home to a golden Buddha that was donated many years ago by a Thai devotee. It is housed in a small shrine in the sand-raked Zen garden. This recipe originally called for just two bananas, but we decided to add an extra one as an offering to our Buddha. Use the ripest bananas you can find, and enjoy plain or with butter.

Heat the oven to 180°C and grease a loaf tin.

Cream the butter and sugar together. Add the eggs and beat until light and fluffy.

Add the sifted flour and the rest of the ingredients and mix together.

Place in the loaf tin and bake for up to 1 hour.

Cover, once cooled, to prevent drying out.

- 125 g soft butter
- 1 cup brown sugar
- 2 eggs
- 1 cup cake flour
- 3 bananas, mashed
- 1 tsp bicarbonate of soda, dissolved in 2 cups warm water
- 1 tsp baking powder
- ½ cup chopped nuts

wholesome and healthy

seeded loaf

(makes 1 loaf)

A yeast-free, nutty and nutritious bread that makes a beautiful loaf without any kneading. Perfect bread-making when time is limited.

Pre-heat the oven to 180°C and grease a loaf tin.

Sift the dry ingredients. Stir in the sugar.

Mix the yoghurt, oil and milk. Combine with the dry mixture and mix thoroughly. Stir in the mixed seeds.

Spoon into the loaf tin. Sprinkle with sesame seeds and bake for 45 minutes.

Switch off the oven and leave for a further 15 minutes.

- 4 cups nutty wheat
- 5 ml bicarbonate of soda
- 5 ml baking powder
- 5 ml salt
- 25 ml brown sugar
- 500 ml plain yoghurt
- 50 ml sunflower oil
- 50 ml milk
- 1 cup mixed seeds (sesame, sunflower, pumpkin, poppy)
- sesame seeds to garnish

Loaf of Bread

this hut with its crusted
floor, walls and roof,
rises from baker's clay
and stone ground flour.

there are holes in the eaves
for birds to nest in,
the ones that twittered
in the wheat fields
and winged above
the threshing barn
to witness the crushing.

cracks open in the walls
to let life breathe within.
sliced into rooms,
it breaks in crumbs of light.

I give thanks to the farmer, harvester,
kneading hands, baker's oven.
as I dwell in this hut and it in me,
it builds floor, roof and walls
of this body, cell by cell,
this seed rich Zen bread.
(DH)

our daily bread

brc brown bread

This bread is made lovingly by the kitchen staff every day. They begin the process of kneading and resting the dough in the early morning. By mid-morning you can smell the delectable aroma of baking bread from far away. A hot loaf fresh out the oven is served with lunch, and at night another is enjoyed with the evening soup. What is left over from the day before is toasted and served with the usual breakfast fare. And just as one cycle of bread-making ends, another begins, ensuring that there is always the perfect loaf to accompany every meal.

Combine the dry ingredients in a large mixing bowl.

Add enough water (approximately 2 cups) to make a stiff dough.

Knead for 10 to 15 minutes until elastic.

Cover with a clean dish towel and allow to rise until doubled in size (approximately 45 minutes).

Knock down and knead for a further minute.

Roll into a sausage shape and place in the greased loaf tin. Cover and allow to rise for a further 30 minutes.

Pre-heat the oven to 180°C and grease a loaf tin.

Bake for 1 hour. For a really crispy crust, turn off the oven and leave for a further 15 minutes. For a softer crust, brush or spray the loaf very lightly with water and cover when out of the oven.

(makes 1 loaf)

4 cups brown bread flour
2 tsp salt
½ packet instant dried yeast
  (5 g)
1 tsp vegetable oil
water (approx. 2 cups)

Tip
For an even lighter loaf, use
3 cups of the bread flour
and 1 cup of nutty wheat.

165

A Long Loaf

I bite into a slice of Ixopo toast
spread with butter and marmalade.
each mouthful stretches a long way.
do the ancestors lick their lips
at the mark of my teeth in the bite?
and the rhythm of my circling mouth?
there are as many of them watching
as there are crumbs in the loaves
rising from today's baking.

each bite is for the hunger
of my mother and fourteen siblings,
my grandmother and her hunger
and thirst for righteousness.
for all the forefathers
who hungered for enough,
such as my grandfather
who looked through a bottle
at the kaleidoscope of his life.
I chew for my father's line –
his brother killed in war,
his sister dying in infancy.

this butter is not scraped thin
but lies thick as curd.
the rind and peel bitter-sweet,
layered rich as an autumn stream,
spill over the edge of the bread.

come ancestors, dip your fingers
in this syrup, lick them clean.
share the gold crust, this family manna.
may you taste fragrance
in lemon and orange blossom.
I bite this bread for all of us.
(DH)

isikhwama bread (perfect pockets)

pita bread

(makes 10 pita breads)

The idea of making your own pita bread may not seem very appealing. True, it is a little arduous, but the final product is very rewarding. Ask a friend to help with the baking as it can be quite a challenge for one person to keep everything going at once. I first made these with Dudu, but it was Nomsa who suggested the title for this recipe when she casually congratulated us for making perfect little bags (*isikhwama*) entirely out of bread. The name stuck and I am happy to say that the results were enjoyed by all, hot out the oven, with generous slatherings of butter. Delicious!

1 sachet instant dried yeast
  (10 g)
3 cups warm water (approx.)
1 tsp brown sugar
3 cups cake flour
1-2 tsp salt
¼ cup sesame seeds
  (optional)
olive oil

Place the yeast in a small mixing bowl. Add 1 cup of warm water and the sugar, and stir until the sugar is completely dissolved. Stand for 15 minutes until the water is frothy.

Sift the flour and salt in a large mixing bowl. Stir in the sesame seeds. Make a well in the flour and add the yeast liquid. Gradually add the remaining 2 cups of water until a thick dough is formed. If there is too much water, add a little more flour.

Knead for 15 minutes until smooth and elastic.

Place in a large bowl lightly greased with olive oil. Rub the surface of the dough with olive oil and allow to rise until doubled in size (approximately 3 hours).

Once the dough is ready, turn out onto a floured surface and divide into equal portions (roughly the size of a tennis ball). Roll lightly into balls, cover and rest for a further 10 minutes.

Preheat the oven to 225°C.

Roll the balls one at a time on a floured surface. A thinner dough will create a better result so aim for no thicker than 5 mm. Place the pockets on floured baking sheets and bake in small batches for 6 minutes, turning once they start to puff.

Allow to cool on a tray for 2 minutes, and then place immediately in freezer/bread bags.

Tip
Can be stored up to 3 days. Warm in a hot oven for 2 to 3 minutes just before serving.

The view that wasn't there

It was November 1969. I was driven around all day by an estate agent, looking for a property somewhere in the Natal Midlands which I could develop into a meditation centre. Nothing had gelled. My funds would only buy ten or twenty acres, which clearly was far too small for my purpose. Somewhat larger properties at my price were either hemmed in by chicken farms or very remote and inaccessible. Then the rain came down. Thick mist descended. So we decided to dry out at the *Off-saddle Inn* in Ixopo, have a cup of tea and go home. It did not look promising.

I chatted to the owner of the hotel, Franz Lupke, who said he had exactly what I was looking for: 300 acres. I said that was too big; it would cost too much. But he said that it would be very cheap. It was. He had been trying to sell it for years, but nobody wanted it because it was useless for farming. It was too steep, too hilly. But it might be just what I was looking for.

Despite the pelting rain and mist, he insisted on showing us the land.

After a twenty minute drive in his clapped-out Land Rover, we came to a slithering halt at the end of a muddy path through a wattle plantation. A farm gate was faintly visible in the mist a few metres away. Franz leapt out of the car beckoning us to follow him. He had vanished in the mist, but I could hear him yell that there was a lovely view further on.

In a daze, I walked towards the gate, instantly soaked to the skin in the deluge. As I stepped through the gate I heard myself say: "OK, I'll buy it!" It was now Franz' turn to be incredulous. "Really?" "Yes," I said.

I came back the following week in bright sunshine to look for that lovely view.

There it was – just a short walk from the gate.

The cooks and contributors

Louis van Loon purchased the property on which the Buddhist Retreat Centre has been established in 1970. It opened for its first retreat in April 1980. In this recipe book he recalls some of the incidents in its early history and describes some of the retreats he conducts there. During the 1970s and 80s he lectured in Buddhist philosophy at the universities of Cape Town and Durban-Westville. His interest lies in the psychology of meditation and in the relationship between art, science, religion and philosophy. He is an architect and consulting civil and structural engineer in private practice.

Chrisi van Loon was in charge of the editing of this recipe book, as she was with its predecessor, *Quiet Food*. She oversees and generally directs the many activities at the BRC, including the setting up of the retreat programmes and liaising with teachers. She sources the exquisite merchandise for the BRC shop. An excellent cook, a vegetarian and animal lover, she ensures that the BRC keeps its reputation for producing fine vegetarian food.

Daniel Jardim joined the BRC in 2007 after spending 10 years in the UK where he studied Holistic Nutrition. He became a vegetarian at an early age and explored vegetarian cooking over many years. Under his tenure as the chef in charge of the BRC kitchen, he introduced his recipes to the BRC menu, many of which are featured in this book. Visitors to the Centre often gave him standing ovations. He trained the women in the kitchen to become cooks in their own right. He now teaches cookery workshops independently as well as at the BRC during which he encourages people to become more holistically aware of the food they consume.

Beatrice Dlamini

Beatrice has worked at the BRC since August 1995. Guests frequently ask her about the secrets of the dishes they have just savoured and she is always ready with a list of spices and ingredients. Beatrice is sensitive and creative in her culinary skills. She has recently qualified as a sangoma.

Francisca Dlamini

Francisca is known to everyone as "Fra". She joined the BRC staff in January 1997. She helps with cleaning and is an imaginative cook.

Lindiwe Ngcobo

Lindiwe is one of the three chefs of the BRC and joined us in 1993. With her beautiful heart and sensitive palate, she is one of our three food magicians. Quiet in nature, she imparts a touch of class to all her culinary creations.

Rosemary Ngidi

Rosemary became a member
of the BRC staff in January
2000. She was trained by
Daniel, and has gained a
particular skill in making
desserts. In addition, she helps
to keep the Centre's rooms in
immaculate condition.

Lungile Mbona

Also trained by Daniel,
Lungi is known as our
"Dessert Queen". She
joined us in October
2007 and quickly became
our chief dessert chef.
Perhaps it is testing all
those sweets that gives
her that constant smile
and cheerful nature. In
her spare time, Lungi
enjoys sewing.

Manene Nene

Manene prepares lunch
for our Zulu staff
members who enjoy her
traditional recipes. Her
pap and spinach are
legendary. In addition,
she works in the laundry.
She has been with us since
February 1994.

Nomusa Mthembu

Nomusa joined us in January 2000. She soon became the chairperson of the staff committee by unanimous vote. She is Head of Cleaning and Laundry, but also helps with bread-making and other kitchen duties. She is a qualified sangoma.

Dudu Memela

Trained by Daniel, Dudu is the third of our top three chefs and has been with us since January 1994. Everyone is now familiar with Dudu's delicious Moroccan couscous, a specialty of the BRC. She has an eye for presentation and transforms the BRC buffets into colourful feasts for the eye as well as the taste buds.

Zaphi Xaba

When Zaphi joined us in January 1996, she worked in the forest with the late M. Mbanjwa, our Induna. She now works in the kitchen and helps with cleaning duties. She is always cheerful and friendly.

Angela Shaw knew taking photos made her happy when, age 16, she saved up for a Nikon FM. Hours were spent in the darkroom and the alchemy of processing and printing in the dark and quiet honed the composition, highlight and shadow of her image making. Her career started on *The South China Morning Post* in Hong Kong. Since then she has produced work for two sell-out exhibitions and numerous publications and private commissions, including the first *Quiet Food*. Angela continues to work on photographic projects she loves from her base in Durban.

Claire Clark counts herself lucky. Her passion for all things creative has become her career. Being a freelancer, she has collaborated with many talented people and worked on a variety of design projects. She feels blessed to have been part of *The Cake the Buddha Ate*. Her journey has taken her into many aspects of design, from fine art to graphic, painting to photography, layout to styling. She is inspired by living in Durban and its luscious natural environment. To her, food is one of nature's finest creative designs.

Stephen Coan is a journalist on *The Witness*, Pietermaritzburg's daily newspaper. He has been involved with the Buddhist Retreat Centre both as a retreatant and teacher for over twenty years. Out of this experience came his collection of poetry, *Chant of the Doves*. He has also published two books arising from his research into the life and work of H. Rider Haggard. His poems feature in this recipe book (SC).

Dorian Haarhoff is a writer, story-teller and mentor. Passionate about developing innate creativity and imagination, he believes in the power of images and stories to spread loving kindness and to bring healing; to build our belonging. He is a former Professor of English (Namibia). Dorian's poems appear in *Quiet Food*. He draws his inspiration from the literature, mythology, narrative therapy, spirituality, and eco- and Jungian psychology – and from frequent visits to the BRC. Like the tingshaw, the Retreat Centre echoes through his poetry which features in this recipe book (DH).

Acknowledgements

A special thank you to Sarah Woods and Chantel Oosthuizen for proof-reading the manuscript and improving the presentation of the recipes.

To Anthony Shapiro for creating the exquisite ceramic bowls and platters on which the BRC food is displayed.

To Chantel Oosthuizen and Junaq Atkinson for collecting the biographies of the BRC kitchen staff.

To Tomas Campher for the photographs on front cover,
pp ii, 4, 36, 98, 116, 122, 150.

Rodney Kidd for the photograph on page 92.

175

Also published by the Buddhist Retreat Centre, Ixopo

Quiet Food: A Recipe for Sanity

Index